Columbus Ghosts

Historical Haunts of Ohio's Capital

Robin Smith

muses
writing
design
editing

P.O. Box 1264, Worthington, OH 43085-1264
emuses@columbus.rr.com

Edited by Jennifer E. Poleon, with assistance from Amber Stephens.
Design by Robin Smith.
Cover photo by Greg Bartram/Better Image Photography.
Ink-wash illustrations by Kathy Murphy.
Interior photos by Robin Smith except where indicated.

Printed and bound in the United States of America
Published by **Emuses Inc.**
P.O. Box 1264
Worthington, OH 43085-1264

ISBN 0-9723153-0-6

5 4 3 2 1

Contents

For my mother, Rosemary Stinson Beard, and
my grandmother, Clora Clark Stinson,
who will never know
what they started.

Preface: Collecting Ghosts

I've been collecting ghosts since

—as they used to say—I was in short pants. Naturally, I started with the classic campfire tales that kept me and my fellow campers awake for half the night at various Girl Scout and church campgrounds. The first "real" ghost story I remember hearing happened when I was eleven years old, on the night my maternal grandmother died. My mother and I had been staying at her house; during the night Grandma, who had been fighting cancer for some time, took a serious turn for the worse. An ambulance was summoned to transport her to the hospital. My grandfather and aunt went with her, while Mom stayed at the house with me.

Later that night, Mom awakened to see my grandmother standing at the foot of the bed. She didn't speak, just stood there for a few seconds, then disappeared. Later when my grandfather and aunt returned to the house with the news that Grandma had died, Mom realized that her vision had occurred at about the same time as my grandmother's death.

Although I found the story rather frightening as a child, Mom always found Grandma's appearance comforting, as she did later in vivid dreams when Grandma would advise Mom about troubling situations in her life.

Let me just say that I come from a solidly blue-collar, no-nonsense family, mostly farmers and manufacturing workers. We are not, as a group, given to high imagination. My parents and grandparents made ends meet through two World Wars and the Great Depression, and like many of their contemporaries, were firmly focused on the practical side of life — making a living and raising their children. But since my mother's vision on the night of Grandma's death, I've heard several other family ghost tales.

The most recent tale happened to one of my cousins shortly after his mother — my Aunt Mildred — died. Mildred was a talker. If she didn't have anyone at home to talk to, she was on the phone to one of her children. Shortly after his mother's death, my cousin John and his sister Cristy had finally sold Mildred's house, sold or divided her furniture and belongings, and were settling back into their normal lives. John had returned to work, on a job that required him to spend a great deal of time in his truck; he carried a pager at all times so he could keep up with phone calls from his office and co-workers. One afternoon his pager went off. Pulling it out of his pocket, John saw a familiar phone number...Aunt Mildred's, now disconnected.

Stories like these from people I know lead me to believe that some ghost stories are more than campfire tales. Are ghosts really disembodied spirits? Are they tricks played by our own minds? Are they emotional imprints that somehow replay themselves over and over? I don't know, but I'd love to find out.

I have never personally SEEN a ghost. I emphasize the word seen because that seems to be the gold standard of belief for many people, but ghost sightings are not nearly as common as auditory phenomena — hearing one's name spoken, footsteps, door knocks, and even the classic clinking chain — and tactile sensations, such as well-defined cold spots in an otherwise warm area, the strong feeling of an invisible "presence," or the sensation of having been touched by an invisible hand. My few personal experiences, one of which is found in this book, fall into those categories — although I'm still hoping!

When collecting the stories in this book, I started, in most cases, with an oral account or newspaper story and worked backward from there. For many of these stories, which are primarily set in public buildings and have been told and retold for many years, it was not possible to find someone who had experienced the story personally. In many cases I was able to speak to someone on staff at the various locations who could confirm the basics of the stories and offer some historic background on them.

For all sites I've also included historical background on the buildings and the people associated with them. Where it was possible to pin down dates of occurrences reflected in the stories, I've searched the microfilmed collection of Columbus newspapers and the history stacks of the Columbus Metropolitan Library and the State Library of Ohio for further background.

In some cases, the names of the people in the stories have been changed where, in my judgement or theirs, it was better not to reveal their real name. These pseudonyms are indicated with an asterisk next to the first use of the name. In the case of "The Grandpa Ghost," the location of the house involved was not given because it is still a private residence and I did not wish to "stigmatize" the house; the location of the building in "A Mansion Needs a Maid" was not revealed at the request of its current occupants.

What I've found in the course of doing research is that it is impossible to "prove" a ghost story—but that wasn't really my purpose to begin with. The ghosts that I've collected here are those whose stories and locations I found interesting and that gave me that little chill down the back of my neck when I first heard them. They speak to me about the passions and events of other times in Columbus, about the wide range of people who have inhabited Ohio's capital—and about the possibility that some of our past citizens have never really left.

I hope you enjoy my collection of ghosts as much as I've enjoyed making their acquaintance.

Acknowledgments

I gratefully acknowledge the following, without whom, etc. etc.

For general inspiration and encouragement, my business partners, Jennifer Poleon and Kathy Murphy, who always thought I could do it; Connie Cartmell, author of *Ghosts of Marietta*, for assuring me that this book was possible; and Kate Matheney of the Columbus Landmarks Foundation.

For research on various sites, Georgeanne Reuter of Kelton House; Kylie Towers of the Kappa Kappa Gamma Heritage Museum; Chuck Bryan for help with Schwartz Castle; Sgt. Jeffrey Sacksteder of the Columbus Police Division Homicide Unit and the Police Division archivists for research on the 1956 Schwartz Castle murders; Dick Stevens and Jeffery Setser of The Elevator Brewery and Draught House; Trish Houston of Thurber House; Lois Neff of the Hilltop Historical Society for help with Camp Chase; and last but not least, Christopher Matheney and Joel Flint of the Ohio Statehouse Education Department — I hope that I haven't damaged your reputations as serious historians.

For marketing assistance, thanks to Sherri Mauger, whose enthusiasm for this project made those last few weeks before publication fun again.

And finally, my husband Brian and daughter Jessica for patiently putting up with my fascination with ghosts and cemeteries when I could be, in Jessica's words, "getting interested in something normal like zoology."

Introduction

Ghost. What do you think of when you hear that word? A filmy white specter on a Victorian staircase? A campfire in the woods and a flashlight left on to keep the dark away? A clink of chains in a quiet graveyard?

Wherever there are people, there are ghost stories. Try it sometime: In a group of people, ask if anyone has had an experience they couldn't quite explain... a glimpse of a figure from the corner of the eye, the whisper of a name in an empty room, the overwhelming feeling that someone is standing near when one is alone. If your friends are honest with you and with themselves, you'll be surprised at how many stories you'll hear.

Some ghost stories are common to many locations, becoming more like folk stories or urban legends, attached to similar sites in many different places. But there are also those tantalizingly specific haunts that are unique to their place, and frequently experienced in the same way by several unconnected people over a period of many years. Are they actually disembodied spirits at work? Pockets of energy left by former occupants? Psychic "movies" imprinted on a place at a time of great fear or stress? All or none of the above?

Whatever answer you choose to believe or not to believe, Columbus is full of fascinating tales of ghosts who haunt cemeteries, theaters, historic homes, military facilities, and government buildings, many of which are open to the public. I hope the following tales give you that delicious little shiver up your neck and raise the hair on your arms — and that they inspire the curiosity to investigate both historical and present-day Columbus. It's a great place to explore the dusty past — and, apparently, to spend eternity. Enjoy.

Johnny Came Marching Home

Oscar Dwight Kelton was 18 years old when
he marched off to the Civil War in 1862 with the 95th Regiment,
Ohio Volunteer Infantry. He and more than 3,000 of his Union
compatriots met death at the hands of Nathan Bedford Forrest's
Confederate troops at the Battle of Brice's Cross Roads near
Guntown, Mississippi on June 10, 1864. Young Oscar did not come
marching home when the war ended 10 months later.

Buried near the battleground where he died, Oscar lay in his
Mississippi grave until his father, Fernando Cortez Kelton, traveled
south after the war to bring his eldest son home. On the way back to
Ohio the wagon overturned, spilling both Mr. Kelton and Oscar's
coffin into the road. In spite of a concussion suffered in this grisly
accident, Mr. Kelton made it back to Columbus to bury Oscar in the
family plot at Green Lawn Cemetery.

A few years ago a Junior League secretary crossed the back garden on her way to Kelton House from her office in a building just to
the north. As she passed the carriage house she saw a young man in a
Civil War uniform leaning against the side of the building. Since the
museum frequently hosts Civil War-era educational programs, she

assumed the man was a reenactor taking a break in the garden—except that there was no such program that day, and no reenactors on the grounds.

Perhaps Oscar, barely a man when he died in Mississippi, made it back to Columbus in soul as well as body—to spend eternity at his boyhood home.

Built in 1852, Kelton House was the home of Fernando Kelton, his wife Sophia Stone Kelton, and their seven children, Anna, Oscar, Ella, Edwin, Arthur, Frank and Charles (who died in infancy). Mr. Kelton was part owner of a lumber company on nearby Livingston Avenue. He was both well-connected and respected in Columbus, serving on the boards of many local businesses and charitable enterprises including the fledgling Columbus School for the Blind. When the body of assassinated President Abraham Lincoln traveled through Columbus, Mr. Kelton was one of 14 honorary pallbearers appointed to accompany the President's body from the funeral train to the rotunda of the Ohio Statehouse to lie in state. Mrs. Kelton was also active in the community, and was one of the founding board of the first Universalist church in Columbus. There is strong evidence that the Keltons sheltered slaves moving along the Underground Railroad; the grandson of Martha Hartway Lawrence, a slave taken in by the Keltons, visited the granddaughter of Fernando and Sophia in the early 1970s, sharing family stories over tea. In 2000 Mr. Lawrence presented Kelton House with a schoolbook that had been passed from the Kelton sons to his family members; both Kelton and Lawrence children had recorded their names in the book.

Fernando died in 1866 after a fall from his office window that was blamed on dizziness from the concussion suffered while bringing Oscar's body home. After Sophia Kelton's death in 1888, first son Frank and then Edwin lived in the house with their families. Edwin and his wife Laura Brace Kelton had five daughters, Grace, Ella, Laura, Lucy and Louise. The Kelton family occupied the house until the death of the last of the daughters, Grace Bird Kelton, on Christmas Eve in 1975. Miss Kelton left the house and all its furnishings to the Columbus Foundation, asking that the house be assumed by an organization that would restore and maintain the house as a museum and decorative arts library. The Junior League of Columbus now operates the house as a museum portraying the home of a well-to-do Midwestern merchant in the period 1850–1900. The Keltons' furnishings and possessions fill the rooms and family portraits gaze down from the walls just as they have for more than 100 years, as though Fernando and Sophia might momentarily return from an afternoon walk.

Visitors who come to Kelton House to admire the gracefully curved front stairway and the antique piano in the front parlor sometimes get to interact with more than the volunteer docents in their period costumes. Sometimes they find themselves the guests of a more ethereal group of hosts.

Georgeanne Reuter is currently the Director of Kelton House. She has been working there since 1983 and has heard many stories about the house from both staff members and visitors. "Some of the people who told me stories are people who wanted to see a ghost so badly they could taste it," she says, "and other people are absolutely surprised by the experience — they had no expectations. Sometimes I think people who want to see a ghost so badly — they see one."

In November 1998, Kelton House hosted a "tell us your ghost story" party and invited staff, volunteers and guests to share their firsthand experiences. These stories were recorded by Reuter at the party.

The Man in the Flannel Shirt

Kelton House is a popular stop on the Columbus Landmarks Foundation's yearly ghost tours. After a 1994 tour, Vicki*, a volunteer docent (whom Reuter describes as a lawyer and a very stable person), a Kelton House staff member and a Columbus Landmarks Foundation volunteer were closing up the house. As the three started down the first-floor hall from the kitchen to the front door, Vicki, who was in the lead, was partially turned around talking to the staff member behind her. Approaching the bottom of the front stairway curving down on their right, Vicki heard a sound like fingers snapping several times; before she could turn her head to look for the source of the sound, she bumped into what felt like a very solid person standing in the hall. She turned to apologize—and found the hall empty. The staff member behind Vicki had also heard the "finger snapping" sound, but the Landmarks Foundation volunteer heard nothing. None of the three saw anything unusual. After briefly retreating to the kitchen, they made their way back down the now unoccupied hall and out the front door.

Asked if she could describe the tactile ghost, Vicki judged it to be a "tallish man," based on the bulk of his "body;" her sense of the man was so real that she could describe his shirt as flannel or some similar soft cloth. "There's no flannel shirt guy in our histories," says Reuter, "so we don't know who the man could have been."

The Watcher in the Window

The southwest bedroom on the second floor is referred to by the staff of Kelton House as "Sophia's bedroom." Bright and airy with its south-facing windows, the room is a focus of ghostly activity in the house. Beth*, newly hired as Kelton House's Special Events Coordinator, was closing up the house one evening soon after starting her job. After locking the doors and setting the security system, she pulled her car out to the end of the driveway and glanced up at the window of the southwest bedroom. There she saw a female figure wearing a black veil gazing out the window. Startled, she first thought that she had locked someone in, but she was sure that she had been alone in the house. Realizing that the figure didn't seem quite solid, she thought perhaps she was seeing some object in the room that only gave the impression of a human shape. The following morning she searched the room, but found nothing that she could imagine looking like the figure she had seen the night before.

Puzzled, she walked back down the front staircase, coming face-to-face with the portrait of Sophia Kelton hanging in the front hall. "That is the person I saw," said Beth, convinced that Sophia Kelton had watched her leave the night before.

On another occasion, Ken*, the boyfriend of a docent, saw the image of a small woman in a dark dress that he described as "very still—translucent, like smoke" in the doorway to Sophia's room. As he watched from the hall, the figure rotated 180° as if on a pedestal—and disappeared.

A former Director, Sally*, looked up as she was talking to a wedding guest in the hall outside Sophia's room and saw a woman walk into the bedroom. Since the museum rooms are not normally open to event guests, she finished her conversation and went to politely ask the wandering guest to rejoin the wedding party. The room was empty, although she had clearly seen the woman enter and no one had come back out. Asked how it felt in the room, Sally said, "It was a very friendly, warm feeling. I felt like there was something there that I couldn't see."

Like a gracious, ghostly hostess watching over her guests.

Ladies of the House

In early January, 2002, a docent led a tour group of schoolchildren through the house. As the children returned to the first floor after touring the upstairs bedrooms, one asked, "Who was the lady in the blue dress upstairs?"

Good question, since the docent was the only person present wearing period dress. Mysterious women are frequent visitors to Kelton House, usually appearing on the front or back stairways or on the second floor. Diane*, Kelton House's cleaning lady, described a woman she saw standing at the top of the front staircase as "small, dressed in black, with a faded face," with her hair pulled back from her face and up, and wearing a period costume.

But the elusive ladies of Kelton House are not always silent specters. About three years ago, the mother-in-law of a bride who had been married at the house the previous weekend called to request reimbursement for cleaning the bride's wedding dress. She said a lady upstairs whom she assumed was a staff member had told the bride to hang the dress in the "closet" on the second floor (actually a wardrobe rack, used at the time to store the docents' costumes). When the dress was retrieved, it had rubbed against something black, soiling the bodice. Understandably upset, "She wanted to know who was that woman who told her to put the dress there," says Reuter, "as if we had some kind of a housekeeper—which, of course, we don't."

Kevin*, curator of Kelton House, once had a gentle encounter with a ghostly female in the attic. At the time the attic was a large unfinished space used to store various items not currently on display in the house. As Kevin was leaving, he whimsically told the house good night. To his surprise, "a very feminine, sweet voice" whispered into his left ear: "Good evening." He interpreted the voice as Sophia's, but was at least positive that he was not just hearing his own thoughts. "When you say things in your own mind," he said, "you hear your own voice."

The Pitter-Patter of Ghostly Feet

The main first-floor hall was certainly a very busy place when Kelton House was filled with children and servants. Evidently some of them are still working on those eternal errands.

Connecting all the first-floor rooms, the hall runs from the kitchen on the north side of the house to the front door on the south side. Near the kitchen, the back or servant's stairway joins the hall on the west side; about halfway to the front door is the base of the formal front stairway. On the east side of the hall are the doors to the front and back parlors.

16

Many people have reported hearing footsteps running in the main hall, says Reuter. "Back in about 1990 I was working on a project on a Sunday. All the other people had left, and I was down here," — indicating the basement meeting room where we sat — "with one of the house managers. We heard a door slam and footsteps right down the hall, then a door slam. It was as if someone had come out of one room, run down the hall, and slammed the front door. I had never told anyone that story until the ghost story party," says Reuter, "but several people around the table had had the same experience." One of the Kelton House cleaning ladies was in the basement when she heard eight distinct steps, going from south to north — so clearly that she could tell when they moved from carpet to hardwood floor. Positive there was someone upstairs, she found no one when she checked.

The Kelton family, from Fernando to Grace Kelton, are buried in a peaceful section of Green Lawn Cemetery, behind and to the right of the chapel. But while their earthly bodies rest in the shadows of the Kelton family monument and the surrounding trees, their spirits seem to be more comfortable in the home they loved. And why not? Surely there are worse fates than spending eternity sharing your home with admiring visitors. So remember, if you visit the Keltons' home, to tell Sophia "Good night." She just may answer.

The Barefoot Fury

Heav'n hath no rage like love to hatred turn'd,
Nor Hell a fury, like a woman scorn'd.
    —William Congreve (1670–1729)

It is a cold, snowy night in February, 1909.

The wind blusters and moans up High Street a few blocks north of
the Statehouse, swirling the snow around the fronts of the buildings.
In the warm light behind the Tiffany-style facade commissioned by
the Bott brothers for their cafe — one of the finest cafes in the U.S. —
Col. Randolph Pritchard enjoys a drink at the bar.

Col. Pritchard is well-known around Columbus — or perhaps infamous is a better word. A paper of the day describes him as "a torrid
womanizer, a noted cheat at cards and a scalawag in business." He is
not a man with whom a respectable woman would be seen.

A message is passed to Pritchard that there is someone waiting to
see him outside. Perhaps he wonders who it is who won't come in out
of the snowstorm that envelops Columbus … or perhaps he knows
who would call him out into the weather rather than be seen
speaking to him in a public cafe. He steps out into the stormy night.

Moments later, he staggers back through the door and collapses on the intricate tile mosaic floor, the blood from a stab wound to the heart spilling across the tiles as he dies. The other patrons throw the door open and rush out to nab the assailant — and find only the bare footprints of a woman running up High Street into the storm.

Some versions of the story say the woman stabbed Col. Pritchard to stop his unwanted advances. Others say she was furious that he had betrayed her trust with another woman. Whatever her motive, she was never caught — at least not by any earthly policeman. But on snowy nights in February, she returns to the scene of her crime, doomed forever to leave her bare footprints in the snow, running up High Street and into eternity.

The ornate stained glass facade with its unique curved windows still stands at the front of the Elevator Brewery and Draught House at 161 North High Street, proclaiming "Bott Brothers Cigars" on one side of the door and "Bott Brothers Billiards" on the other. The interior, too, remains much as it would have been in 1909 — an ornately carved tiger cherry bar and back bar boast intricate wood and mother-of-pearl inlays, as do the built-in display cabinets near the entrance. The Bott brothers, who manufactured billiard tables and bar fixtures, built not only a cafe, but a working advertisement for the quality of their wares. The mosaic floor has also survived the business's many owners, as have the dozens of carved faces — winged, placid, or angry — that are part of the back bar and surrounding woodwork. Current owner Dick Stevens has covered the walls above the antique wainscot in the back half of the restaurant with some of his collection of paintings. One of the paintings portrays the former second-floor pool parlor in its heyday. Now a law office, at one time its 40 pool tables were busy late into the night. Stevens now maintains two antique pool tables, one built by the Bott brothers, in an area at the rear of the restaurant, under a large stained-glass window.

Since the Bott brothers built their cafe in 1905, the space has always been a restaurant or bar. During Prohibition the drinks changed to milkshakes; afterward the place reopened as The Clock Restaurant, named for the large clock that stands on the sidewalk outside. By the 1970s the facade had been boxed in and The Clock had become a seedy downtown bar and pool hall—Ladies Welcome!—but in the 1980s new owners uncovered the Bott brothers' stained glass and The Clock again became a restaurant.

Today the Elevator is a popular lunch spot for downtown workers. And as for otherworldly visitors? Owner Dick Stevens says he hasn't heard about any particular ghostly manifestations. "I don't know of anything that's happened since we've been here," he says, "just the ghost story that everyone has already heard." Office manager Jeffery Setser took me through the basement, a long narrow space divided into several rooms and partly filled with brewing equipment for the Elevator's 12 house-made ales and lagers. Setser says he's never seen anything he couldn't explain in the basement, but in the very back room, which is partly filled by the building's mechanicals, he says some of the staff once thought it would be cool to try out a Ouija board. While not giving any details of the session, he says, "It was pretty scary,"—an experiment that hasn't been repeated. "There's definitely some weird energy in this part of the basement," he says.

At least some of the Elevator's employees are convinced that the "weird energy" is a haunting; overhearing a conversation regarding the story of the barefoot woman, one of the hostesses told me with a shudder, "Oh, yeah. This place has definitely got ghosts, no doubt about it."

Is it the barefoot murderess? Or the unfortunate Col. Pritchard? So far, the ghosts of the Elevator are keeping their secrets.

The Lady in Gray

Imagine waving goodbye to your sweetheart or husband as he marches off to war through the hills of northern Tennessee. Imagine the pain of knowing your loved one is a prisoner in a Union prison camp plagued by overcrowding, disease and cold winter weather. Imagine learning that he has died and been buried there, far away from you and his green Tennessee hills. Would you go to search for him if you could?

After the attack on Fort Sumter opened the Civil War in 1861, Columbus made a rather abrupt transformation from small town to booming state capital. Thousands of troops were mobilized at Columbus, and it became clear very quickly that a sizable Army camp was needed in the area. A site was chosen on the western outskirts, four miles west on the National Road (now Broad Street), that had the requisite roads, water supply, rail lines, and telegraph lines already in place. By 1862, the camp was fully operational, a self-contained city where thousands of Union troops lived and worked. Named Camp Chase in honor of Secretary of the Treasury Salmon P. Chase, a former Ohio governor, the camp occupied the space from Broad

Street south along Hague Avenue to a point between Fremont Street and Wicklow Road. With Hague Avenue as its east boundary, the camp stretched west to the area between Westmoor and Westgate avenues.* In the southeast corner of Camp Chase was a prisoner-of-war camp. At first, the camp was occupied by only a few military and civilian prisoners from Kentucky and Virginia, then by a number of prisoners from the Western campaigns, including enlisted men, officers, and even a few of the officers' slaves. As Union victories increased in Mississippi and Tennessee, the flow of prisoners also grew, and the camp became more and more crowded. The prisoners were put to work expanding the facilities, but at its peak more than 9,000 souls were jammed into facilities designed for 7,000. Streets were wet and muddy and the buildings were cold in the winter. Open latrines and cisterns were breeding grounds for bacteria. Diarrhea, fevers, bronchitis and smallpox swept through the camp, infecting men already weakened by the crowded, uncomfortable living conditions. Thousands of them died there. According to an abstract of the official camp records, there were a total of 2,144 deaths between July, 1862 and July, 1865, but some historians believe the number was actually much higher—perhaps as many as 5,000. Many were taken back to the South for burial, but many others had to be interred in Yankee soil.

At first, the dead prisoners were buried in the old east cemetery on Livingston Avenue (now Livingston Park). After a cemetery was established south of the prison camp, those men were moved back to Camp Chase to join their more recently deceased brothers. Before the war ended in 1865, 2,260 sons of the Confederacy were buried in the

*This area was arrived at by David Roth of *Blue & Gray* magazine and Paul Clay of the Hilltop Historical Society using a surveyed map of Camp Chase by William W. Pollard, Columbus's only surveyor in the period 1861–1866, found by Mr. Roth in the National Archives in Washington, D.C. The process by which they made the determination is described in *The Men and Women of Camp Chase*, which is listed in the sources for this story.

only remnant of Camp Chase still in existence: the Camp Chase Confederate Cemetery on Sullivant Avenue.

Among the rows of identical white gravestones is the marker of Pvt. Benjamin F. Allen of the 50th Tennessee Infantry, who is evidently the object of a woman's devotion that has lasted far beyond this mortal life. For many years, visitors to the cemetery have reported seeing a young woman walking among the tombstones, head down, weeping, as though she is searching for the grave of a loved one. Tall and slender, she wears a gray traveling suit in the style of the 1860s. So absorbed in her search is she that she walks through trees and even through the iron gate at the entrance as though they don't exist — and perhaps in her time they don't. It is said that it is the gray lady who leaves the mysterious flowers often found on the grave of

Pvt. Allen, and occasionally on the grave of the Unknown Soldier at Camp Chase. Is she a wife, a sister, a grieving sweetheart who watched the man she loved march off to a war from which he never returned? And having come this far, what prevents her from being reunited with the man for whom she searches? We will never know. And until she finds the answers, the Lady in Gray will continue to devote herself to finding the man she still mourns for, even beyond the grave.

A Postscript: The Veiled Lady of Camp Chase

Louisiana Ransburgh was born in New Madrid, Missouri on December 10, 1849. After her mother's death when she was 14, she was sent to the Columbus area to live with relatives. She attended Ohio Wesleyan University. In October of 1867 she married Joseph Briggs, a captain in the Union Army and the founder of the village of Briggsdale, south of Columbus.

After the war ended, Louisiana Ransburgh Briggs courageously became the first local woman to pay honor to the thousands of Confederate dead in Camp Chase Cemetery. Risking community disapproval and the censure of friends, Mrs. Briggs would don a long veil and go to the cemetery under cover of darkness to throw bouquets of flowers over the stone wall, becoming known as the Veiled Lady of Camp Chase. Mrs. Briggs continued to live in the Briggsdale area until her death in February of 1950 at the age of 100.

Was Louisiana Ransburgh Briggs the living prototype of the Lady in Gray? Perhaps. Or perhaps the living Veiled Lady and the ghostly Lady in Gray are united only in their desire to honor and to grieve for their Southern brothers, lying in the cold earth so far from their homes.

Ohio's Haunted Statehouse

It's a warm Saturday evening in September of 2000. On the grounds of the Ohio Statehouse, time has rewound to the early 1860s. Tents cover the lawn and men in the blue uniforms of the Union Army cook over campfires. Inside the rotunda of the Statehouse, Union Army officers and ladies in Civil-War era gowns whirl across the floor at the Statehouse Civil War Encampment Ball. As the evening wears on, two teenage boys take a break from the festivities, heading down the stairs to the restrooms on the floor below. Nearing the bottom of the staircase, one of the boys sees the hazy figure of a man standing in a doorway to his right. The man is wearing the long black frock coat of the Civil War era, and has his right hand extended in front of him as though to shake the boy's hand. But as the boy approaches, the man seems to flash past — or through — him and up the stairs. Startled, the boy turns and follows the man up the stairs, but the man has disappeared. "Did you see that man?" the boy asks his friend. The friend has seen nothing.

Construction of the Ohio Statehouse began in 1839 and dragged on through more than 20 years of political intrigue, funding problems and cholera epidemics. Finally completed in 1861, it was immediately engulfed in a national cataclysm — the Civil War. Troops camped on the Statehouse lawn as they prepared to march, and many of the major political and military figures of the era walked its halls, including Generals Ulysses S. Grant and William Tecumseh Sherman and Sherman's brother John, who represented Ohio in both the U.S. House of Representatives and the U.S. Senate. In 1861, Abraham Lincoln was in the office of Governor Salmon P. Chase (later Lincoln's Secretary of the Treasury and Chief Justice of the U.S. Supreme Court) when he received word that the Electoral College had elected him President of the United States. A short four years afterward his body lay in state in the Statehouse rotunda while 50,000 mourners made their way past his coffin.

Considering the intensity and emotion of those first years of the Statehouse's existence, it is not surprising that the building would continue to harbor traces of the Civil War era within its walls — like the mysterious man in the doorway. The most memorable man of the age, Abraham Lincoln visited the Ohio Statehouse several times in bodily form. Some believe he still makes an appearance from time to time, generations after his untimely death.

The Last Dance

In 1859 Abraham Lincoln attended the festivities celebrating the completion of the Ohio legislature's new chambers. A ball was held in the new senate chamber; the hostess was Kate Chase, the beautiful daughter of the governor. The tall, rather disheveled politician from Illinois and the fashionable Miss Chase seemed quite taken with each other as they whirled around the dance floor — an impression not lost on a jealous Mary Todd Lincoln. When she could stand no more, Mrs. Lincoln strode on to the dance floor and ended their dance. Or did she?

Many years later, Joseph B. Foraker, Ohio's governor from 1886–1890, was working late in his Statehouse office. Believing himself to be alone, he was puzzled to hear music from somewhere in the building. Following the sound, he found himself in the Senate members' lounge — and looking through the windows into the Senate chamber saw a beautiful woman in a billowing ball gown and a tall, distinguished man in formal dress dancing in time to the ghostly music, finishing the dance that had been interrupted so many years before.

A Postscript: Kate Chase

The beautiful and vivacious Kate Chase could rightfully grace the pages of more than one collection of ghost stories. The eldest daughter of Salmon P. Chase, Kate became her father's official hostess at the age of 16 and brought both sophistication and a sparkling personality to Columbus's social scene. When the Chases moved to Washington, D.C. during the Lincoln administration, Kate quickly became the center of a large social circle. Mary Todd Lincoln was uncharmed by Kate, and for many years Washington society was split between Mary Lincoln's friends and Kate Chase's friends.

Kate married Senator William Sprague of Rhode Island in the Lincoln White House, receiving a kiss from the President, whose wife did not attend the ceremony. The marriage was not happy. Sprague — perhaps rightly — came to believe that Kate had married him for his money. There were allegations that Kate had one or more lovers, and rumors that Sprague abused her. Soon after her father's death, Kate moved back to Salmon Chase's home and Sprague sued for divorce, gaining custody of their young son. With no husband to support her and very little money of her own, Kate sank into poverty, shunned by her former friends and deserted by her alleged lover. Late in her life she was reduced to raising chickens and selling their eggs to make money.

Kate Chase Sprague died in 1899. Her three daughters by William Sprague escorted her body back to Ohio, where she was buried next to Salmon Chase at Spring Grove Cemetery in Cincinnati. Her ghost is said to haunt the cemetery, always wearing a pink dress—her trademark color. She also supposedly haunts the downstairs rooms of the White House, disappearing when spotted but leaving behind the scent of lemons and spices.

A Most Dedicated Public Servant

In the nearly 150 years since Lincoln's day, the Ohio Statehouse has changed with the needs of the state government. An annex, originally planned to house the Supreme Court and currently used for Senate offices, stands on the east side of the original structure. The Statehouse interior has been remodeled repeatedly to provide additional office space; by 1989 there were 317 rooms, compared to the original 53. A seven-year restoration finished in 1996 removed 225 rooms, re-opening the light courts that provided illumination during the Civil War era and reviving the building's sense of grandeur. Through the years thousands of legislators, judges, governors, and state employees have carried on the business of the state under the Statehouse roof. Of course, some of them were more dedicated than others...

Thomas Bateman was appointed a Senate message clerk in 1919 and named Clerk of the Ohio Senate in 1927. He remained in his post for more than 50 years, retiring in 1971. Mr. Bateman earned a reputation as a straightforward, meticulous, do-it-by-the-books man who was often consulted by legislators on points of parliamentary procedure and legislative process. He held a law degree from The Ohio State University and was regarded as an authority on Ohio constitutional law. As methodical in his habits as he was in his work, Mr. Bateman left his office each day at the same time, through the same door, taking the same route through the halls of the Statehouse. And although he died in June of 1981, members of the Statehouse staff who remember his precise habits say some part of Thomas Bateman still lingers in the building where he served the State of Ohio for so long.

For every day, precisely at the proper departure time, a cold chill emerges from Mr. Bateman's former office. Lights dim and flicker as the chill passes — down the hall, down the stairs, across the rotunda, out the door — and Tom Bateman's ghost heads home for the evening.

34

The Thurber House Ghosts

It is perhaps Columbus's best-known ghost
story: "The Night the Ghost Got In," by James Thurber, a hilarious
encounter between the author, his brother and mysterious late-night
footsteps pacing the dining room. Hilarious, yes, but also based on an
actual occurrence at Thurber House, where James Thurber lived with
his family from 1912 until 1917. Thurber told the real story in unpub-
lished notes found among his papers after his death.

Thurber's nonfictional encounter with a ghost took place during
his junior year of college — around 1912. Late one night as Thurber
was upstairs washing his face before going to bed, he heard heavy
footsteps circling the dining room table on the first floor. The
thought of a ghost did not occur to him; thinking there was an
intruder in the house, he woke his brother and they went to the
head of the staircase leading from the second floor to the dining
room below. As soon as they reached the head of the stairs, the
sounds stopped. Thurber's brother, not having heard the footsteps,
asked Thurber what the matter was. Thurber declared loudly that
there was someone walking around on the first floor — and suddenly
the footsteps began again, this time rushing up the staircase toward

the two young men. Terrified, Thurber's brother ran for his bedroom and locked the door. Thurber held his ground until one more step would have sent the invisible presence rushing into him, then instinctively slammed the door at the head of the stairs shut.

Thurber, then a fledgling journalist, set out to solve the mystery of the footsteps. He asked the local druggist, who had been in the neighborhood for many years, if he had ever heard of anything unusual at 77 Jefferson Avenue. The druggist, surprised that Thurber had never heard the story, proceeded to tell him about the mysterious footsteps earlier tenants had heard circling the dining room.

Thurber tried sleeping downstairs several nights, hoping for a ghostly repeat performance, but never again heard the footsteps. He did turn up a possible explanation: Years before, a man who then lived in the house had received an anonymous phone call at work. The unknown caller told him that if he went home at 10 a.m. and entered quietly through the kitchen, he would find his wife and her lover at his house. He did so, and after pacing around the dining room several times in agitation, rushed up the stairs and shot himself in an upstairs room.

Perhaps coincidentally, the date Thurber gives for his encounter, November 17, is the anniversary of a tragic event that took place in the same area: the Ohio Lunatic Asylum fire. Jefferson Avenue was originally one of three circular, park-like streets built on the former site of the Ohio Lunatic Asylum, which opened in 1838 with a capacity of 140 people and expanded over the years until by 1848 the complex held more than 450 people. The 30-acre grounds of the asylum were a popular picnic place for the citizens of Columbus during the 1860s, although some of its neighbors were beginning to call for removing the asylum to a site further from the growing city. On the snowy evening of November 17, 1868, an attendant noticed smoke coming from one corner of the east dormitory wing. With most of the residents gathered in the main hall for a night of recreation, much of the staff joined all three of the local fire companies to battle the fire, which quickly raged out of control. A lack of water and the snowstorm and cold temperatures forced a decision to abandon the building. Rescuers pulled most of the residents to safety, but in the area where the fire originated, 32 women were trapped in a series of rooms with no escape route. Firefighters climbed to the roof of the burning building, cut holes, and managed to pull 26 of the women out; six others died before they could be rescued. Perhaps their souls have never left.

Whatever the origins of the busy spirits of Thurber House, it appears that the perpetrator of the heavy footsteps is neither gone nor alone. Esther Reich, who rented two rooms of the house from Anna Bancroft during the late 1930s, often heard footsteps running up the back steps, dismissing them as noises from a neighbor's house. However, a year or two after moving to other quarters, she came back to visit with her former landlady and encountered a visible presence. She spent the night in the alcove, a small area off the living room. Awakening suddenly from a sound sleep, she saw a figure sitting in a rocking chair in the corner. The figure was an image of a person in despair, hunched forward with his elbow on his knee. She laid back down for a second, sat up again, and the figure was gone.

The most recent reports of ghostly events come from Thurber House writers-in-residence, who live in the third-floor attic apartment during their tenures. Some are prankish: a closet door that refuses to stay closed, a radio that switches stations while turned off, a burglar alarm tripped by — whom? Other writers have closer encounters.

Paula DiPerna, writer-in-residence in the spring and summer of 1988, saw the ghost as she stepped out of a car in the parking lot behind the house. She said, "I happened to look up to the apartment and the ghost — a hefty, somewhat stooped, black torso shadow, apparently dressed in a raincoat with the collar turned up, moving at a silhouette's pace — made a single pass through the hallway lights just as my eyes travelled up the building wall, as if waiting there, set in motion by my glance." DiPerna asked Donn Vickers, then the director of Thurber House, to walk her upstairs — where they found the apartment empty.

Laurie Hertzel was a journalist-in-residence during the summer of 1994. She said she noticed closet doors that seemed to open and close themselves and heard unexplained footsteps on the second floor, but never saw anything. However, her dog Toby twice encountered something in the house, invisible to Hertzel but quite apparent to Toby.

The first time dog met ghost, Toby had been asleep at Hertzel's feet in the writing room. He woke up, wandered into the living room, stopped suddenly, and began to growl. When Hertzel followed, she found Toby, body rigid, staring at one of the chairs and growling ominously at — no one. "I called his name. I grabbed his collar. But I couldn't break his concentration." Finally, she broke the spell by throwing a tennis ball down the hall.

A few weeks later, Hertzel was browsing in the bookstore one evening while Toby meandered from room to room. Again, Hertzel heard Toby growling; she followed him to the parlor and found him with eyes fixed on the gold velvet sofa. "This time, his growls were bolder, punctuated with a few sharp warning barks. I tried to walk to the couch to see if there was something there that had caught his eye, but he cut in front of me to keep me away." Then the growling stopped, as though Toby's antagonist had vanished. "He approached the couch cautiously, and sniffed it in a perplexed kind of way, but whatever it was seemed to be gone."

Thurber's mysterious man in the night? One of the unfortunate inmates of the Ohio Lunatic Asylum? The return of the despairing figure in the rocking chair? We may never know. Only one thing is certain — the spirits are many and restless at Thurber House.

All ghost stories and quoted material are from *The Thurber House Organ*, Autumn 1988. My thanks to Trish Houston of the Thurber House staff.

The Man of Mystery

The grave is a cold, dark place, cut off forever
from the warmth of the sun. But one well-known German Village
resident who loved the sun during his mortal life may have found his
way back from beyond the tomb to catch a few rays.

A red-brick house with a distinctive eight-sided tower looms over
the east side of South Third Street just south of Livingston Avenue.
This German Village landmark was built in the mid-1800s by Dr.
Frederick Wilhelm Schwartz. Dr. Schwartz was a well-known
Columbus apothecary who owned a successful shop at East Main and
5th streets and taught the pharmacy trade to George Karb, later the
first German mayor of Columbus. The house, nicknamed the
Schwartz Castle, was built for Schwartz's betrothed, who remained in
Germany. However, she never came to the U.S.—some say she sent
Schwartz a "Dear John" letter; many say she declined to come because
she thought Frederick Wilhelm Schwartz was insane. Schwartz lived
in the house as a bachelor for the rest of his life, sometimes sharing
the house with his mother and two sisters.

For many years, Schwartz was referred to in Columbus as the
"man of mystery" due to his eccentric habits. According to an article

published in *The Columbus Citizen* the day after his death on May 11, 1914, "Rumor had it that he was an astrologer, a chemist, a mystic, but he was none of these. His strange actions were caused by an extreme love for nature and all things pertaining to it." His "strange actions" included eating no meat, drinking only rain water, grinding his own grains and cooking his own food. He generally went barefoot, let his hair grow long, and, despite his career as a druggist, never touched any drugs or medications. His most famous habit was sunbathing in the many-windowed tower of his "castle" or on its roof—sometimes in the nude.

Schwartz's house was as eccentric as its owner. The octagonal tower that dominates the front of the house may have been modeled on a structure remembered from his native Germany. On the north side of the top story of the tower was an iron spiral ladder providing access to the tower's roof. The interior walls of the house were tiled, the stairways made of iron, reportedly because Schwartz considered them sanitary. None of his neighbors ever set foot in the Castle until shortly before his death, when a Mrs. Bowers entered the house because she had not seen him in some time and was—correctly—concerned that he might be ill. Those who visited the house during his illness discovered quotations from Shakespeare, Goethe, Heine and Schiller written on the walls and ceilings, some in English, some in German.

It was in the tower sun parlor of his home that Dr. Schwartz passed away at the age of 78. And it is in the sun parlor with its many windows that people report seeing a man bearing a strong resemblance to Dr. Schwartz, with his long hair falling around his shoulders or blowing in the wind, climbing the spiral ladder to take one more sun bath on the roof of his castle.

A Checkered History

After the death of Dr. Schwartz, his beloved castle was bought and sold many times. His sister Louisa tried to buy it at a sheriff's auction shortly after her brother's death, but the sale was later set aside and the house was purchased at auction for $3,755 by Benjamin Manley, a real estate dealer, in 1915. In 1917 the Castle became the Columbus Maternity Hospital. The *Columbus Sunday Dispatch* described the house in some detail on November 4, 1917:

> There are 15 rooms in the building, each having expensive tile as flooring. French plate glass windows costing nearly one thousand dollars at that time, were used on the first and second floors, but the upper story was never finished. It has been said that Dr. Schwartz ordered all work stopped after an unfortunate love affair.
>
> Under the building is a cellar and sub-cellar. The object in having the sub-cellar has never been ascertained.
>
> …Another peculiar feature of the building is that all stone used in the foundation of the building was dressed on all four sides.

The Columbus Maternity Hospital was characterized as "the most completely equipped hospital of its kind in Central Ohio."

As the years went by and the character of the neighborhood changed, Schwartz Castle began a long downhill slide. Always regarded as odd and unique, the Castle began to take on a more sinister reputation. As the small trees planted by Dr. Schwartz matured, only the top of the mysterious tower could be seen from Third Street. There were rumors of a human skeleton in the carriage house — true rumors, as it turned out, but the skeleton was a medical specimen owned by Dr. Schwartz and once found at his drugstore. Stories circulated that the sub-cellar was where Dr. Schwartz had "buried his victims" and described the iron fence surrounding the house as "arrows of Satan." By the mid-1950s, the house had been divided into a number of apartments; the neighborhood was rough — and Schwartz Castle finally lived up to its morbid reputation.

In June of 1956, Eugene Courtney Smith and his brother Farley Smith traveled from Chicago to visit their parents, who lived in a one-room apartment on the third floor of the old Castle. One night during the visit Eugene asked to borrow Farley's car, but Farley refused because his brother had been drinking. An argument ensued, which ended when Farley stabbed Eugene in the abdomen with a butcher knife. The police found Eugene dead on a bed in the apartment after receiving an anonymous call from a woman that there had been a stabbing at the address. Not realizing the seriousness of the wound, Mrs. Smith had attempted to bind it using adhesive bandage strips—too little, too late.

Then in December of the same year, death once again paid a visit to the Castle. Ernest Eaton, who also lived on the third floor with his wife and daughter, purchased two used jackets from his neighbor Sybil Smith, the mother of Eugene and Farley. Eaton claimed to have mistakenly given her a 20-dollar bill instead of a one. Mrs. Smith refused to return the money. The argument boiled over on a second-floor landing the next day when Mrs. Smith reportedly slapped Mr. Eaton's married daughter, who was going downstairs to call the police to settle the dispute. A melee on the landing ended abruptly when Mrs. Smith's husband Raleigh shot Mr. Eaton in the back of the head with a 12-gauge shotgun, killing him instantly.

Six months, two bloody murders, two ghost stories added to the Castle's long and checkered history. It is said that the two murdered men have been seen wandering the building, on the stairs and in the basement. One might wonder if they've encountered each other in their visits and what kind of conversations they might have.

Since the 1950s, Schwartz Castle's fortunes have improved dramatically. With the restoration of the German Village area, the neighborhood improved dramatically and the area became a trendy location for both businesses and residents. After having sat empty and boarded up for a number of years, Schwartz Castle was purchased and renovated in the early 1980s. Robert Echele, a property manager, and Robert Gease, a general contractor, remodeled the first two floors as office space and the upper story as living space, which they occupied for several years. As this book is published, Schwartz Castle is again on the market, but this time as a beautifully renovated property in a desirable area of Columbus.

And the ghosts? Perhaps they still visit from time to time, or perhaps, as is sometimes the case, the more recent renovations have driven them away. But if future tenants should encounter a long-haired, strangely insubstantial man climbing the spiral ladder to the roof, it is to be hoped that they'll let him be. After all, there's sun enough for everyone on the tower at Schwartz Castle.

The Pink Lady

Kappa Kappa Gamma is a fraternity for women —
not a sorority, as some people might assume. Founded in 1870, the
group emphasizes leadership, philanthropy, academic success and
social opportunity. The Kappa Kappa Gamma Foundation provides
scholarships, emergency financial aid to members, and, especially,
educational and leadership programs, many focusing on the changing
roles of women in higher education. The Kappas are a caring, sup-
portive sisterhood, watching over their members and alumnae and
ready with a helping hand.

How appropriate, then, that Kappa Kappa Gamma should have
a spectral "caretaker" watching over visitors at their headquarters
in Columbus.

Phillip Snowden built his Italian Villa-style home in the period
from 1851–1852, when East Town Street was THE fashionable
neighborhood in which to build his "tasteful mansion." Snowden
was a merchant who dealt in silks and embroidery; his wife, Abigail,
ran a millinery business — an unusual degree of independence for a
lady of her class and time. Unfortunately for the Snowdens, a business

downturn forced Mr. Snowden to declare bankruptcy in 1860 and their beautiful home was sold at a sheriff's auction.

During the Civil War era, the house was leased by the State of Ohio and used as the residence of Governor David Tod and his family. Ladies in hoop skirts and gentlemen in frock coats danced past the twin marble fireplaces on the east wall of the the formal parlor and the elite of government officials raised toasts in the formal dining room.

In 1869, the house was purchased by David Gray, whose family owned it for more than 50 years. In 1872 a fire destroyed the original bell tower and part of the second floor; the Grays rebuilt, adding more bedrooms and the distinctive belvedere that now graces the house. After the Grays, a succession of owners used the home as a boarding house, an organizational headquarters (to the back of the house, the Columbus Women's Association added an auditorium, one of the largest in Columbus in the 1920s), a rental property, and finally in the 1930s and 1940s, a poorly kept rooming house, divided into one-room apartments and filled with the odors of heavily spiced food cooked in the open fireplaces. At one time there was a candy factory in the formal parlor.

In 1951, Clara O. Pierce, then the executive director of Kappa Kappa Gamma, was searching for a suitable building for the organization to use as a headquarters and meeting space. She looked at the old Snowden-Gray House at the suggestion of Grace Kelton, whose home a few lots down Town Street was built at about the same time. Seeing the potential of acquiring near-downtown office space and accommodations for visiting volunteers, Kappa Kappa Gamma bought the property and began the task of renovating the building into a functional office facility.

In 1965 another fire struck, destroying most the the office area; the original house sustained heavy smoke and water damage. Undeterred, the Kappas took on the cleanup, rebuilding their offices and repairing the damage to the old mansion.

By 1975 the building was listed on the National Register of Historic Places, along with the Historic East Town Street neighborhood. In 1980, Kappa Kappa Gamma incorporated The Heritage Museum, and after many years of research and fundraising, in early 1991 they set to the task of restoring the front three rooms to their Civil-War era glory.

And what a task it was. Somehow David Gray's 1870s pier glass in the parlor had survived intact. During renovation, layer upon layer of wallpaper was removed from around the huge mirror, revealing only Phillip Snowden's original wallpaper behind it—evidence that the pier glass had never been moved from its position between the twin fireplaces on the east wall. The 400-pound mirror was hanging by its one original wire.

Miraculously, much of the plaster crown molding and many of the ceiling medallions had survived the fires and previous interior changes. They were cleaned and repaired; reproduction carpets, milled in England in patterns available in 1860–1870, were installed. Craftsmen painted faux marble surfaces in the main entry hall and stairways and hand-grained the doors and stairway to look like expensive hardwoods—popular decorating styles among the Victorian elite. Appropriate wall and window coverings and furniture were acquired, including a beautiful period piano for the parlor. Today the house shines as the Heritage Museum, a beautifully restored mansion which also includes guest rooms for visiting Kappas and the Kappa offices, rebuilt, at the back of the building.

And the ghost?

In the early 1900s, the Snowden-Gray mansion was owned by the Columbus Women's Association, and used as their clubhouse. During that time, Celinda Hatton oversaw the upper rooms, which were rented to boarders. Miss Hatton was a talented portrait artist; her self-portrait hangs over the sideboard in the formal dining room and a portrait she painted of her brother hangs over the fireplace. Miss Hatton also ran a respectable establishment and was known for taking good care of her tenants. Legend notes that she often walked through the house in her pink robe to make sure everything was in good order before retiring.

According to Kylie Towers, the archivist and museum curator for the Heritage Museum, the best-known ghostly encounter occurred during the 1970s. "Kappas are notorious for holding marathon meetings," says Towers. "Since a committee may have volunteer members from all over the United States and have only one or two opportunities in a year to meet in person, they'll start at 8:30 in the morning and go until 11:30 at night." During one very late council meeting, the women took a brief break, all putting on their pajamas and robes before returning to the dining room to continue. "When they returned, the secretary called roll to make sure everyone was back, and they all were," says Towers — but then, who was the woman in the pink robe several of them had just seen walk past the doorway in the main hall? Hurrying into the hall, they found it empty; no woman in a pink robe was to be found in the house.

There have been other brief glimpses of the Pink Lady over the years. Is she still making her late-night check of the house and the tenants under her roof? One hopes so. After all, someone has to keep watch over the Kappas as they keep watch over their own.

The Grandpa Ghost

How would you feel if you discovered you were
sharing your home with a stranger? And not just any stranger, but one
from another time, who appears only when the veil between his world
and yours thins and allows a brief meeting? A frightening thought for
many. But all hauntings are not alike...

The red brick houses of German Village were built to shelter the
families of the German immigrants who worked at the nearby
breweries. During the past 25 years many of these sturdy homes
have been rehabbed and updated, but the neighborhood retains the
warmth of its red-brick, working-class origins — and maybe some of
its former occupants, as well.

    Beth Ervin has lived in Columbus and in the German Village area
for many years. Several years ago she shared a three-story brick home
on South Fifth Street with another woman. The roommate occupied
the front bedroom on the second floor, while Beth used the back bedroom. The top of the wooden steps from the first floor was visible
from the door of Beth's bedroom.

One night when her roommate was out of town on a business trip, Beth was lying in bed reading around 10:30 or 11:00 in the evening when she heard footsteps climbing the stairs from the floor below. "I wasn't afraid," she says. "I knew it couldn't have been my roommate, but I really wasn't scared." Looking out into the hall, she saw a man standing at the top of the staircase. "He was an older man, tall, thin, and dressed in work clothes. A baggy shirt, and not jeans, but work pants. He had gray hair and kind of a craggy face." She recalls that the man appeared perfectly solid. "It wasn't like an apparition. He looked real." As the man looked at her from the top of the stairs, Beth says she felt a very warm, comforting feeling from him. "I felt very protected and safe." The man stood there for about 90 seconds, Beth guesses, although it seemed longer at the time — and then he was gone.

"I called him Willard because he made me think of my grandpa, my mother's father, whom I never met." Beth says. She had seen a couple of photos of her grandfather, who was a carpenter. He was tall and thin and probably would have worn work clothes similar to those of the man on the stairs. At first Beth thought perhaps the man was her grandfather visiting her, but later decided that he was probably someone who was attached to the house. She saw the man on the stairs on one other occasion within a few months; again, he climbed up the steps as she lay in bed, stood looking at her from the top of the staircase, and disappeared. "I never saw him again while I was living in that house," she says, "and I've never seen him since I moved." Figuring that if the man were really her grandfather he would have appeared to her in other places, she now thinks that he was possibly someone who had lived in the South Fifth Street house at one time.

Whoever the man on the stairs was, Beth had no fears about sharing the house with him. "He was nice," she says. "I felt so safe."

The Restless Dead

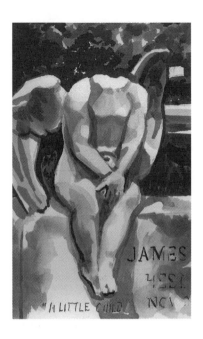

"A LITTLE CHILD" JAMES ...NCY

It is late night in the Short North; the bars and restaurants have closed and the streets are quiet. Suddenly, the faint light of a lantern appears, bobbing down a street in the area of the North Market. The lantern sways in the hand of a man who is dressed in a rather unusual style, as though he has just arrived from the early 19th century. He appears to be searching for something with his pale light. Then, in the blink of an eye, he is gone, his tiny light quenched. John Kerr has still not found his earthly body, lost more than 150 years ago.

When the town of Columbus was formed in 1812, there were as yet no churches or churchyards in which to bury the town's dead. The four proprietors of the city dedicated a tract of land north of the town plat for use as a burial ground in July of 1813. The 1½ acre plot was in a wooded and somewhat swampy area beyond the end of High Street at what is now the corner of Park and Spruce streets. Due to a lack of established authority in the new town, the tract was not offi-cially deeded to the city until 1820 — by John and Mary Kerr, who held title to the land at that time. The Kerrs received one dollar for the land.

Because the North Graveyard was the only burial place in Columbus through the 1820s and 1830s, it was necessary to acquire more land to accommodate the needs of the growing town. By the mid-1840s the graveyard covered the area from Spruce Street south to the area of the railroad tracks south of Convention Center Drive, and from Park Street—which at that time did not curve to the east as present-day Front Street does, but continued straight south along the line of today's Park Street—east to High Street. The opening of the new South Graveyard (later referred to as the East Graveyard) on Livingston Avenue in 1841 and the Catholic Cemetery at Washington and Mt. Vernon avenues in 1846 made further expansion of the old burial ground unnecessary.

By 1848 the growth of Columbus to the north put a new kind of pressure on the old burial ground: as the city grew, not only was the graveyard occupying valuable land, but there was concern about the health aspects of interments so close to populated areas. The opening of Green Lawn Cemetery south of the city in 1849 was the beginning of the end for not only the North Graveyard, but the East and Catholic graveyards as well. The City Council attempted to prohibit further burials in the North Graveyard in 1856 but was defeated by citizens who had bought lots there and were understandably not happy that the city wanted to forbid them to use their lots but was unwilling to make compensation. It was not until 1862, when Green Lawn offered to exchange lots in their new cemetery for those held at the North Graveyard, that the problem was solved. The old burial ground was closed to new burials in 1864.

The final blow to the graveyard was the formation of the Union Depot Company in 1868. Within three years after its formation, various railroad companies had begun to file lawsuits to condemn and vacate parts of the graveyard to provide access to Union Station. Other businesses were also eager to buy land so close to the railroad terminal. By 1885, all the remains had been moved from the old graveyard—at least those that could be found in the graveyard's sometimes sketchy records. John Kerr was among those who could not be located.

Will his wandering ghost ever find its former shell, left behind so many years ago? Clearly his remains were not the only ones lost in the forgotten graveyard; in 1913 five boxes of additional remains were found during construction work and moved to Green Lawn, and in May of 2001, 31 more burials were uncovered during sewer work on Spruce and Wall streets. Perhaps one day the mortal clay of John Kerr will be found. Until then, he will continue to wander the Short North, looking for his bones by the light of a pale lantern.

Rest in Peace—For Now

The North Graveyard is probably the best-known "forgotten" grave-yard in Columbus, but it is certainly not the only burial ground in the city to be overtaken by progress, and not the only place where the remains of some of the occupants were left behind.

The East Graveyard was located on Livingston Avenue at 17th Street. Burials began there in 1841, when it was referred to as the South Graveyard. The area was frequently used for the burial of paupers, including the dead from the county poor house. In 1862 and 1863, 22 Confederate soldiers who died in the prison camp at Camp Chase were buried there, then later removed to the Camp Chase cemetery. By 1873, the East Graveyard was said to be in deplorable condition. In 1875 the City Council began working with the Franklin County commissioners to find and purchase a tract of land outside the city to use for burials and a pest house, to be used jointly by the city and the county. A 30-acre tract was purchased for a new South Graveyard, east of High Street, roughly between St. Rte. 104 and Kingston Avenue. The city closed the East Graveyard to new burials in 1876 and requested the families of those buried there remove their remains from the old burial ground in 1877 in anticipation of either selling the land or converting it to park use. In 1881 the old East Graveyard became South Park, later renamed Livingston Park.

Records from 1881 showed 2,344 graves in the East Graveyard; by September of 1882 1,850 removals had been recorded, but there is no record of a final tally of the number of bodies exhumed and reinterred elsewhere. A number of tombstones apparently remained in the park in 1959, when they were dumped in Alum Creek to help stabilize the banks during a flood. It is possible that many of those tombstones were replaced at the new gravesites, and thus never moved. But it is likely that many of those laid to rest in the East Graveyard rest there still, under the laughing children on the playground at Livingston Park.

Haunting the Halls of Academe

Mysterious disembodied voices. Books that fly off counters. Lights that turn on and off by themselves. A ghostly mother and child in a basement room. Not what you'd expect from a thriving college campus built in the past 30 years — but Columbus State Community College on the northeast of downtown has a reputation for hosting visitors of a most unworldly sort.

The campus police have often been the victims of unexplainable pranks: several officers were standing outside their station talking when the lights on their truck suddenly started flashing, the switch flipped to "On" even though no one was near the vehicle. Another officer was startled when every light in the library suddenly came on one morning at 3 a.m. — and then shut off again.

The ghostly incidents seem to increase when there is construction of any kind on campus. Odd? Maybe not.

In 1846, the Catholics of Columbus purchased land for a Catholic cemetery. Located at the southeast corner of Meadow Lane and the Alum Creek Road (later Washington and Mt. Vernon avenues), the cemetery served the church of St. Remegius and later Holy Cross

Catholic Church, the first in Columbus to support a resident pastor. By 1851, Holy Cross had outgrown its building and in 1853 the Irish minority in the congregation dedicated a new church, St. Patrick's, on Naghten Street. The two congregations continued to share the cemetery, which from its founding had been divided into Irish and German sections (in its only listing in a city directory in 1862, the cemetery is listed as two separate entities—the Irish Catholic Cemetery and the German Catholic Cemetery—at the same address). Despite attempts by the City of Columbus to halt burials within city limits in 1856, the graveyard was in use until Mt. Calvary Cemetery on the West Side was consecrated in 1874.

In late 1887, Columbus Catholics were advised to remove family members from the graveyard, as the Church intended to sell the land. However, no sale was made and in 1905 the land was put to new use as the site of St. Patrick's High School.

And the faithful in the old burial ground? According to different sources, there were anywhere from 1,700 to 4,000 burials in the graveyard; Mt. Calvary's records show only 50 transfers, all from the German section. The first of the remaining bodies were quickly dis-covered during excavation for the high school, when horses broke through two caskets in one morning—the first of many accidental exhumations. The bones that were brought to light during the build-ing of the high school were blessed and reburied at Mt. Calvary. In 1925, when the new Aquinas College High School was built on the site, many more bodies were found. And when Columbus Technical Institute, now Columbus State, began building there, more graves were revealed with each new project. Rhodes Hall, Madison Hall, Eibling Hall—all sit directly on top of the old burial ground.

Eternal rest, it seems, is relative—and the awakened dead are grouchy. If you're on campus late at night, whisper a prayer for the displaced souls there. They weren't expecting a wake-up call.

The Return of Thurston

Green Lawn Abbey rises in Gothic splendor

from the top of a hill near the intersection of Greenlawn and Harmon avenues. An enormous, imposing mausoleum, it seems strangely out of place among the commercial and industrial buildings in the area and the trailer park next door, as though Dracula's castle had appeared next to the local convenience store.

Green Lawn Abbey LOOKS haunted. Its columned facade and locked doors seem custom-made for wandering spirits and a magnet for those who wish to prove to themselves that the dead CAN return. Can they? That's a question that Green Lawn Abbey's most famous "resident" hoped to settle after his death…

Howard Thurston was born in Columbus on July 20, 1870. As a child he was fascinated with the stage magicians who came to perform at Columbus theaters. When The Great Herman visited Columbus young Thurston played hookey to see his show and was thrilled when the magician caused a brass button to appear from his young fan's forehead. Thurston kept the button; from that day his goal in life was to be a great magician.

As a youth Thurston worked as a bellhop at the Neil House hotel at the corner of Broad and High streets, learning card tricks from many of the guests and practicing magic in his spare time. He became a touring magician, well-known for his skill with cards. In 1908, Harry Kellar, then America's most famous magician, retired and sold his show and tricks to Thurston. Thurston spent the next 20 years as one of the country's best-known magicians, becoming famous for large illusions such as the "floating lady" and the Indian rope trick.

Thurston was a friend and contemporary of Harry Houdini and Harry Blackstone. The three magicians and other friends including writer Arthur Conan Doyle also shared an interest in spiritualism and the question of whether the spirit survived after death and could be contacted by the living. As master illusionists, the men were well aware that many mediums were outright frauds; Houdini in particular was relentless in exposing fake visitations from the next world.

During the years before he died, Thurston made pacts with 24 relatives and friends, including his wife, his daughter Jane, and his friend and business partner, Claude Noble, that he would try to contact them "from beyond" at specified places and times after his death. When death came to Thurston the Magician on April 13, 1936 at his summer home in Florida, those with whom he had made pacts began quietly carrying out their instructions.

Thurston's body was returned to Columbus for interment in Green Lawn Abbey, which was then only a few years old and an appropriately impressive last resting place for Columbus's famous son. Thurston's mortal remains were placed in a crypt labeled simply, "Howard Thurston — Magician" with his birth and death dates.

On April 13, 1937 at 12:30 p.m. — one year to the minute after Thurston's death — Claude Noble and William Thurston, the magician's brother, knelt in front of Thurston's crypt, Noble holding a magician's wand. Having recited the Lord's prayer, Noble addressed Thurston: "Claude and your brother Bill are here in accordance with our pact. Manifest yourself if God is willing." Noble and Thurston had agreed that if Thurston's spirit could manifest itself, it would knock the wand from Noble's hand. Noble waited for a full minute, watching the wand closely.

After a minute had passed with no sign of Thurston's spirit, Noble and the small group of people with him quietly left the mausoleum. He was quoted in the *Columbus Evening Dispatch* for April 13, 1937:

> Howard always believed that the spirit is vibration. He never felt it was a voice or the return of the body, but a vibration — a communicative feeling strong enough to grasp something out of your hand and throw it to the floor. He always told me that if he could knock it from my hand in one minute that would be a manifestation of his spirit. Why didn't I wait longer? Howard always said, "If I can do it, I can do it like that!" and then he'd snap his fingers.
>
> Sorry? Of course, I'm sorry, but I'm not disappointed. I'm not a spiritualist, I was simply fulfilling Howard's wishes. If I had died first, he would have done the same for me.

Despite Thurston's failure to fulfill his pact a year after his death, Noble remained hopeful. He told the *Dispatch*, "As long as I live, I will come to Howard's grave on the anniversary of his death and try again. Some day, someone will come back and I'd like it to be Howard." Noble was as good as his word, returning each April 13 for nearly 25 years.

Has Thurston's spirit ever returned to Green Lawn Abbey? Noble never indicated that his friend had made contact, but he never gave up hope. In recent years, other enquiring minds have made the trek to Thurston's crypt in the hope that someday, his spirit will manifest itself. And who knows? Perhaps someday the wand will fall and the spirit of Thurston will at last walk the halls of Green Lawn Abbey.

STATE PENITENTIARY,
, OHIO.

The Screams of the Dying

Late at night when the city is quiet, you can
still hear the sounds near Spring Street and Neil Avenue: The roar of
flames shooting up four stories high. The metallic blows of sledge
hammers and pickaxes on locks — desperate attempts to break open
doors. The screams of men in agony, trapped in iron cells stacked six
high with no escape from the inferno.

It is said that hauntings are often brought about by highly traumatic events, events that leave their imprint on a site forever. On
April 21, 1930, one such event happened in Columbus — the Ohio
Penitentiary fire, a raging inferno that left 322 men dead from flames,
smoke and falling debris. Started deliberately in an effort to cover a
planned escape attempt, the fire resulted instead in hundreds of
permanent discharges from prison life — and an eternity of reliving
that awful night.

The fire began with a crude setup of candles, wood, oily rags and
wood shavings. The plan was for the candles to burn down and ignite
the other materials, starting a fire around 4:30 in the afternoon — the
inmates' dinner hour, when they would be gathered in the dining

hall. The scheme took a disastrous turn when the candles took longer than expected to burn down; the fire didn't take hold until around 5:30, when all the prisoners were locked in their cells. The prison was in the process of an expansion, and the fire quickly reached wooden scaffolding set up by workmen near six tiers of cells. The cell block became a flaming death trap.

There was confusion among the guards, who had no clear instructions on what to do in such an emergency. By the time orders came from the warden to release the prisoners, it was nearly impossible to reach the top tiers of cells. Inmates as well as guards made heroic rescue efforts; one prisoner released 25 men by breaking the cell locks with a sledge hammer. Others grabbed keys from the guards and freed dozens of men from the upper tiers. One convict, called "Wild Bill" — his last name seems to have been in dispute — saved 12 men before dying in the flames. Several of the trapped men chose suicide over death by fire, some drowning themselves in their water basins, two cutting their own throats. One inmate left a poignant note before his death from suffocation: "Gus Socha. Notify John Dee, 93 Armory Ave., Cincinnati."

The April 22, 1930 edition of the *Columbus Evening Dispatch* quoted the reactions of some of the surviving prisoners. One man, searching through the dead in the prison yard for his cellmate, said to a nearby Catholic priest, voice shaking, "Christ above! We're human! We ain't rats! Why did they have to die like this, Father?" Another, reacting to a fellow prisoner comparing the catastrophe to a war, replied, "The war! Don't try to tell me this was like the war! I seen both, brother. Over there, we had a chance for our lives. We had two legs and could run, if we couldn't fight. But not here. There was nothing to do but go crazy, cooped up in a box while they watched the fire coming after them. There was nothing to do but scream for God to open those damned doors. And when the doors didn't open, all that was left was to stand still and let the fire burn the meat off and hope it wouldn't be long about it."

The Ohio Penitentiary was demolished in 1998, freeing the land it had occupied since 1834 for redevelopment. But will it ever be free of the screams of dying men? Only time will tell...

Shadow Pictures

Even before the great fire, death was, of course, no stranger to the Ohio Penitentiary. Starting in 1885, all executions performed in the state took place in the Annex, the far east side of the East Hall building. Until 1896 the mode of execution was hanging, using a scaffold attached to the interior wall of the building. The condemned man (no women were hanged in the Ohio Penitentiary) stood on a trap door. A hood was placed over his head and the noose around his neck. When the trap was released, the man plunged to the end of the rope, inches from the floor below, where the prison doctor would monitor his heartbeat until it stopped. According to *The Historical and Illustrated Ohio Penitentiary* by Marvin Fornshell (published in 1908), it took from five to 28 minutes for a man to die by hanging. It was neither a humane nor a neat way to die — strangulation, his tongue protruding. Although the hood would theoretically cover the man's face, many times it was knocked loose by the force of his fall. In a few unfortunate cases, the rope nearly beheaded its victims when it arrested their fall. Twenty–eight men met their Maker at the end of a rope in the Annex. One was only 16 when he died; two were black men; all made the ultimate payment for their debt to society.

After 1896 the State of Ohio began using the electric chair for executions. The chair was set up directly beneath the trap for the old scaffold; whether by hanging or electric shock, the condemned prisoners died in the same place. Strapped into the chair with a black hood covering his or her head, the victim was dead within a minute after the warden threw the switch. The electric chair took the lives of 315 men and women before its use was temporarily halted over questions of constitutionality in the 1960s. During that period, it was moved to the Southern Ohio Correctional Institution in Lucasville, where it remains.**

Three hundred and forty-three people executed; three hundred and forty-three souls wrested from their earthly bodies. It is to be hoped that most were released to their ultimate destinies in the next world. But the story is told that in the prison's later years, those who had reason to enter the room would often see, swinging slowly to and fro on the wall beneath the old gallows, the shadow of a hanging man.

Bloody Island

Not far from the old Ohio Penitentiary site is a small island in the middle of the Scioto River. The island, formed by a sand bar, was once much larger than it is today. It was called British Island by some

---

**The death penalty was reinstated in Ohio in 1981 after several attempts by the General Assembly to draft a law that would adhere to strict constitutional guidelines. In 1993 Ohio's death row inmates were given a choice between electrocution and lethal injection; on November 21, 2001, Governor Bob Taft signed a bill eliminating electrocution in Ohio. Since 1981 no inmates have been executed by electrocution and three by lethal injection.

and Bloody Island by others, due to an incident early in the history of the Columbus area.

On October 4, 1813, William Henry Harrison's troops defeated British forces at the Thames River in Canada. The great Shawnee war chief, Tecumseh, was killed during this battle, a decisive moment in the War of 1812. Afterward, the island in the Scioto River is said to have been used as a prison for British soldiers captured during the battle.

Desperate to escape, a number of the British soldiers attempted to swim from the island to shore; the American guards shot many of them as they swam.

And even today, it is said that the British soldiers' screams — and perhaps the splash of water — can be heard at night, floating up from the dark waters of the Scioto.

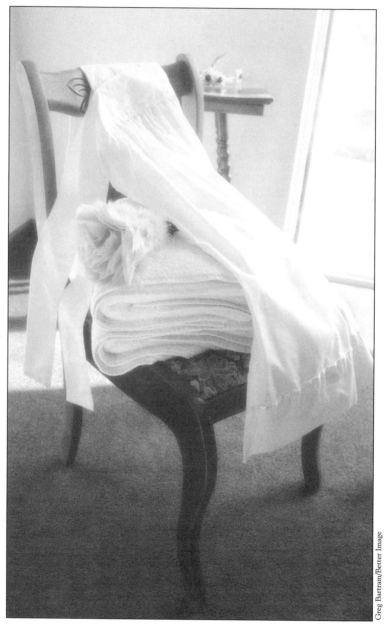

72

A Mansion Needs a Maid

The stately mansion on East Broad Street has
stood for nearly a century. It has housed a wealthy businessman,
several Ohio governors, Ohio's archives, a design firm, a hairdresser,
a restaurant, and several philanthropic organizations.

It also harbors a ghost.

At the turn of the century, Charles H. Lindenberg was the president
of the Lilley Regalia Company, the world's largest manufacturer of
uniforms, badges, emblems, ceremonial swords and other products for
fraternal organizations. Mr. Lindenberg wished to build a home for his
family that would reflect his status in the community. To design his
home, he hired Frank Packard, a nationally-known architect who
designed many of Columbus's best-known buildings including the
Seneca Hotel and the old Memorial Hall on East Broad Street and
the Green Lawn Cemetery chapel. The result was a stunning
Georgian Revival Eclectic brick home trimmed with stone, which was
completed in 1904. The impressive interior featured a sweeping stairway in the main hall that climbed to a huge window, then divided to

lead to the second floor. The walls were paneled in rich woods; large leaded glass windows and a skylighted palm room brightened the house; a ballroom occupied the entire third floor, giving guests more than ample room to dance.

In 1917, the Ohio Legislature passed a bill allowing the state to buy and maintain a residence for the governor. An Executive Mansion Board was formed, which bought land on East Broad Street intending to build a residence — but when the board found that the Lindenberg home was for sale, they purchased it instead. The next home to the east was also purchased and razed to create space for a formal garden. The first of 10 governors to occupy the remodeled and newly refurnished mansion was James Cox in February 1920; the last was Frank Lausche. In 1957 the governor's residence was moved to the former mansion of Malcolm Jeffrey in Bexley. The Broad Street mansion became the home of the Ohio Archives, which remained in the building until the summer of 1970.

By the late 1970s the home had become the Old Mansion Restaurant. One morning in the fall of 1979 the manager of the restaurant was working in her office. At about 10:30 a.m. a customer called to make a reservation. As she wrote down the information the manager glanced up and was startled to see an unfamiliar black woman wearing a blue dress walk past the window of her office. She quickly finished the phone call and stepped out to check the hallway where the woman had been walking. She found no one, and had not heard the heavy door at the end of the hall open and close.

Frightened by now and fearing an intruder, the manager called her boyfriend. When he arrived she let him in — the outside door was locked — and he searched the building, but found no one.

Another restaurant employee, a waiter, often felt a strong presence where the main staircase divides. Although he never claimed to have actually seen the woman, he had a clear mental picture of her as a woman wearing a tight-bodied gown in the style of the early 1900s, with her hair in a bun. He felt the presence several times, and always

74

felt that it was a happy presence. Another waiter, Edward*, saw the woman twice. The first time he had a brief glimpse of a tall woman dressed in a servant's gown walking on the staircase. Edward's second encounter with the woman was in the den, a small room off the main living room. He was setting tables when the woman appeared in the room — and spoke. Edward was quoted in the November 1980 issue of *Ohio Magazine*:

> You ask me how I know she was a servant. I know because she *told* me she was a servant. She said she was happy about what was happening, happy that the Mansion was again being used by people... She had on the same gown, and was pretty, gentle and didn't mean harm."

Others have encountered the maid in the blue dress; visitors to the mansion have also reported mysterious cold spots in the staircase area, where the woman is usually seen. A design firm which once occupied the building was repeatedly beset by a strong smell of burning hair that filled the lobby at the same time every afternoon. The smell lingered for about 20 minutes, then dissipated. Suspecting an electrical problem, the owners had the wiring checked but found nothing. Other occupants also have reported the burning hair smell, as well as loud "sonic booms" that shake the house — but are not heard or felt elsewhere in the area.

The current occupants of the building are aware of the stories but say that they have had no unusual experiences since they've been there. Perhaps the mansion maid is satisfied at last that her beloved home is in good hands.

Drill Hall and N. C. Officers' Quarters,
Columbus Barracks, Ohio.

Ghost Soldiers of Fort Hayes

April, 1865. Ohio, along with the rest of the nation, is plunged into mourning by the assassination of Abraham Lincoln only days after the surrender of General Robert E. Lee at Appomattox Courthouse in Virginia. Lincoln's funeral train passes through Columbus, where the body of the late President is escorted to the rotunda of the Statehouse to lie in state. The commander at the Columbus Depot, a military installation on the northeast side of Columbus, orders an hourly cannon salute during the time that Lincoln's body is in the city.

Even in the face of national tragedy, however, the intrigues and small plots of daily life continue. The commander's daughter has been showing too much interest in a handsome young private under her father's command — a man her father believes to be an eminently unsuitable match for his beloved daughter. As the cannons fire again and again, one begins to show signs of dangerous overheating. The commander assigns a certain private to the overheating gun. At the next salute, there is a deafening roar as the gun explodes, killing the young man instantly.

A tragic accident, or the ultimate solution to the commander's problem? The commander and his daughter have long since taken the answer with them to their graves. But the young private's soul still lingers at Fort Hayes, perhaps hoping for a last word with the young woman whose father sent him to his death.

The construction of what is now Fort Hayes began in 1863, at the height of the Civil War. The government purchased the land intending to build a new arsenal to supplement the old arsenal building on Main Street. Formerly known as "Neil's Woods," the land had been owned by Robert Neil, whose family also once owned the land where The Ohio State University was built. The entire area was covered by mature oak trees, many of which had to be cleared before construction began. The first building completed at the site, now called the Shot Tower, was designed for the safe storage of weapons and munitions and was never actually used to manufacture shot. Today the Shot Tower is the sole remaining Civil War-era building at Fort Hayes; most of the current buildings date from a period between 1880 and about 1920.

The "General's House," built in the 1890s, seems to be the favorite haunt of the unfortunate young private. Doors open and close for no apparent reason, and visitors to the basement of the house report encountering an unnatural cold there. One painter working in the building during renovations left and refused to return after repeatedly hearing footsteps in the house and finding no one else in the building.

The young private is not the only ghostly presence wandering the grounds of the old fort. The installation, officially called the Columbus Barracks after about 1880, had grown considerably by World War I, sporting a large Post Exchange, a Receiving Station for new recruits, a YMCA, a hospital that was considered one of the best in Columbus, quarters for officers, non-commissioned officers, and enlisted men and a large park with a bandstand where public concerts took place during the summer. In 1910 a drill hall was built for indoor exercise and drill training. It was also used for movie screenings and other recreational purposes.

The Columbus Barracks was an active recruiting and training post in every war fought by the U.S. after the Civil War, and was used heavily for reserve training during World War I. Renamed Fort Hayes in 1922, the post was also an induction center after the Selective Service Act was passed in the 1940s. It was during World War II that a young soldier guarding the fort fell asleep at his post. Brought up on charges of dereliction of duty, he was confined to the jail near the drill hall. While awaiting trial, the soldier was found dead in his cell of unknown causes.

Dead, yes, but not gone. Perhaps hoping to atone for his neglect of duty, the young soldier has been seen for many years in the vicinity of the Drill Hall. Those who have spotted him say he appears nervous and disappears suddenly, as though he realizes he has been seen.

Although some of the military buildings at Fort Hayes are still used for storage and by local military units, most of the buildings have been declared surplus by the government and stand empty and rotting. The Columbus City Schools acquired about half of the site, renovating the Shot Tower for use as an alternative arts school — a curious parallel to the other Arsenal building on Main Street, now the Cultural Arts Center. The Columbus schools also make use of several other buildings, including the General's House. However, the Drill Hall, the Company C and Company A quarters, what is left of the officers' quarters and many other buildings stand empty and vandalized, sheltering only transients, area wildlife — and the spirits of the men who lived and died there.

The Castle Ghosts

Just east of the Main Street Bridge over the
Scioto River, the Cultural Arts Center stands over Bicentennial Park
like a miniature medieval castle with its corner towers and walled garden. The Columbus Recreation and Parks Department offers gallery
space and public art classes in the facility, making use of its open
spaces and many windows. But the building and its site have not
always been used for such creative and enlightening activities — and
it's just possible that some of its past lingers on into the present.

For years, students have claimed that they've seen a hazy woman
in 19th-century dress materialize among the work tables in the pot-
tery room, a low, one-story addition to the Center on the west side of
the building. Sometimes only her upper body can be seen, and her
face is never clear. Why is she there? No one knows, but the students
have nicknamed the apparition Esther, for an unfortunate woman
who paid the price of a life gone wrong nearby.

In February, 1812, the Ohio legislature called for the construction
of a state penitentiary, choosing a 10-acre site in the southwestern
area of the new borough of Columbus. On a modern day map, the
prison grounds would cover roughly the area from the intersection of

Rich Street and Civic Center Drive south to I-70 and west to the river. The first penitentiary building was erected in 1813, followed by a second in 1818, when the original building was remodeled into quarters for the warden and his family. The inmates were kept busy manufacturing a variety of goods which were sold to help offset the cost of the inmates' incarceration. But discipline was lax. There were frequent fires in the facility, and overcrowding quickly became a problem. In 1832 the state legislature decided to start fresh with a new prison, to be located in Franklinton. Male prisoners were moved to the new building in October of 1834; the new women's building opened in 1837.

The former penitentiary site was mostly unused for many years as lawsuits and countersuits over the ownership of the land made their way through the courts. However, the county sometimes used the site as a "hanging hill." One infamous execution was that of James Clark, who murdered a prison guard with an axe in 1841, and Esther Foster, a black woman who beat another female inmate to death with a fire shovel. The two were publicly hanged on February 9, 1844 at the southwest corner of Mound and Scioto streets. The occasion drew a large, unruly crowd of both men and women; many in the crowd were drunk, and in the confusion and disorder a man was trampled to death by a horse. If it is true that spirits can be tied to a place by a traumatic death, it would be no surprise if Esther's ghost lingers, unable to leave the site of those last bitter moments of life.

Even after the lawsuits were settled in favor of the state, the area remained largely empty for good reason: In the early to mid 1800s, the south side of Columbus was a low-lying, swampy area filled with tanneries, rendering plants and other foul-smelling enterprises. The Scioto River was essentially the city's garbage dump; in the 1850s the city built its first underground brick sewer to carry waste to the river — which was carried over the Columbus feeder for the Ohio and Erie Canal in an open aqueduct before dumping odoriferously into the Scioto at the south edge of town.

But in the mid-1850s, there arose a great deal of tension between native-born Americans and recent immigrants, including the many Germans who settled in the areas now known as German Village and the Brewery District. In response to these tensions, the state of Ohio thought it prudent to use the old penitentiary site to build an arsenal and armory for the Ohio Militia. Fortunately, the militia never had to intervene between the Germans and the longer-standing citizens of the city. However, the arsenal building was used heavily during the Civil War, and was still in use as a National Guard armory until 1975.

Today, the Cultural Arts Center is surrounded by parkland, offices and high-rise buildings filled with expensive, well-appointed condominiums—a far cry from the days of tanneries, raw sewage and citizen unrest. But perhaps there are some holdovers from a more colorful, less genteel past.

There is the curious incident of the elevator. Bill*, a longtime instructor at the Cultural Arts Center, was in the building late one night working on a personal project. "It was about three o'clock in the morning," he told me during a break from a class, "and I had been in the building alone for hours. I heard the elevator start up downstairs." It came up to the floor where Bill was working and stopped, the doors opened—and the empty elevator sat there as though waiting for someone to board for a trip to—where? "I packed up my things and left. By the stairs! No way was I getting on that elevator," Bill said with a wry smile.

Finally, there is the presence in the basement. Several years ago I was a student at the Cultural Arts Center, taking a life drawing class in the evenings; at the time this incident happened, I had been taking classes for several months and was very familiar with the building, but had never heard of anyone having a ghostly encounter there.

At a class break one evening, I took the elevator down to the basement vending area. I was the only person who made the trip to the basement. I got off the elevator and turned right to the soda machines around the corner, then came back to await my return ride.

After I pressed the elevator button, I looked around curiously. The basement was very low; from the elevator it ran off in three directions, each section vaulted by a low, arched ceiling. I had been told that there were some children's programs held in the basement during the summer, but it appeared that the area was mostly used for storage, with the spaces dimly lit and filled with odd bulky shapes and boxes. I turned back to check the elevator button and suddenly felt the hair on the back of my neck rise with the feeling that there was someone else in the basement watching me. I pushed the elevator button again; the feeling of a presence behind me quickly grew so strong and felt so close that I was afraid to turn and look over my shoulder. Fighting panic by now, I punched the button again, and was considering whether I should make a break for the staircase when at last I heard the elevator coming down from the floor above. I glanced behind me as the doors closed and saw... nothing. But the invisible presence had been so palpable and so unexpected that I was still shaking when I got back to my class.

Director Jennifer Johnson said in response to an inquiry about ghost stories connected with the building that she really didn't know of any. "We joke around about it," she says, "but we really don't have any."

Ghost stories are like that — elusive, fascinating, tough to track down and impossible to prove. Are ghosts real? Certainly many people — sane, sober and sensible folk — believe that they are. For myself, I am quite certain that I encountered something in the basement of the Cultural Arts Center; I felt its presence as surely as I would have if another person had come up behind me. Was it a ghost? I don't know, but I'll admit that I hope so.

Curious? Stop by the Cultural Arts Center sometime; admire its unusual structure and enjoy the galleries and the bustle of people from all over the area making art. And if you happen to spot a woman in the crowd who seems a little, well, insubstantial, be sure to wave hello.

Sources

Johnny Came Marching Home

http://centralohio.thesource.net/Museums/keltonhist.html, November 21, 2001.

http://www.ohiocivilwar.com/cw95.html, November 8, 2001.

http://www.americancivilwar.com/statepic/ms/ms014.html, January 25, 2002.

http://www/itd.nps.gov/cwss/Personz/Detail.cfm?PER_NBR=2027511, November 8, 2001.

Interview with Georgeanne Reuter, director of Kelton House, January 10, 2002.

Lee, Alfred E., A.M. *History of the City of Columbus, Capital of Ohio, Vol. II.* Munsell & Co., New York and Chicago, 1892.

Lentz, Ed. *As It Were: Stories of Old Columbus.* Red Mountain Press (no city), 1998. ISBN 0-9667950-0-8.

Lubrano, Alfred. "Local spooks leave some haunting tales," *Columbus Citizen-Journal,* Friday, 31 October, 1980, page 17.

Samuelson, Robert E. et al. *Architecture: Columbus.* ©1976, The Foundation of The Columbus Chapter of the American Institute of Architects, Columbus, OH.

Thomas, Robert D., ed. *Columbus Unforgettables: A Collection of Columbus Yesterdays and Todays.* Robert D. Thomas, 1983.

Woodyard, Chris. *Haunted Ohio: Ghostly Tales from the Buckeye State.* Kestrel Publications, Dayton, OH, 1991. Ninth printing, 2000.

The Barefoot Fury

http://www/elevatorbrewing.com, January 9, 2002.

Interview with Jeffery Setser, office manager of The Elevator Brewery and Draught House, January 15, 2002.

Miller, Alan. "Tour to follow ghostly footprints," *The Columbus Dispatch,* 18 October, 1988, page 1C.

Taylor, William Alexander. *Centennial History of Columbus and Franklin County, Ohio, vol I.* The S.J. Clarke Publishing Company, Chicago-Columbus, 1909.

Woodyard, Chris. *Haunted Ohio III: Still More Ghostly Tales from the Buckeye State.* Kestrel Publications, Dayton, OH, 1994. Second printing, October 1995.

The Lady in Gray

http://www.cwc.lsu.edu/cwc/projects/dbases/chase.htm, March 4, 2002.

http://www.civilwarhome.com/campchase.htm, March 4, 2002.

http://www.geocities.com/Pentagon/Quarters/5109/history.html, March 4, 2002.

"100-Year-Old Briggsdale Woman Dies," *Columbus Citizen*, February 27, 1950.

Clay, Paul, Patti Ongaro and Lois Neff, comp., *The Men and Women of Camp Chase*. The Hilltop Historical Society.

A Centennial Biographical History of The City of Columbus and Franklin County Ohio. The Lewis Publishing Company, Chicago, 1901.

"'Grandma' Briggs, 100, Dies After Color-Filled Ohio Life," *The Columbus Dispatch*, February 27, 1950.

Lentz, Ed. *As It Were: Stories of Old Columbus*. Red Mountain Press, 1998. ISBN 0-9667950-0-8.

Thomas, Robert D., ed. *Columbus Unforgettables: A Collection of Columbus Yesterdays and Todays*. Robert D. Thomas, 1983.

Switzer, John. "Flowers add to ghost story," *The Columbus Dispatch*, Sunday, 29 October, 1989.

Switzer, John. "Lady in gray has her haunts," *The Columbus Dispatch*, Saturday, 28 October, 1989.

Woodyard, Chris. *Haunted Ohio: Ghostly Tales from the Buckeye State*. Kestrel Publications, Dayton, OH, 1991. Ninth printing, 2000.

Woodyard, Chris. *Haunted Ohio IV: Restless Spirits*. Kestrel Publications, Dayton, OH, 1997. First edition, 1997.

Ohio's Haunted Statehouse

Interview with Christopher Matheney, site manager, Statehouse Education and Visitors Center, and Joel Flint, historian, Statehouse Education and Visitors Center, February 22, 2002.

The Ohio Statehouse Self Guided Tour (booklet).

Oscard, Anne. *Tristate Terrors*. ©1996 by Anne Oscard. Hermit Publications, Dayton, OH.

Thomas, Robert D., ed. *More Columbus Unforgettables: A Further Collection of Columbus Yesterdays and Todays*. Robert D. Thomas, 1986.

The Thurber House Ghosts

Interview with Trish Houston, director for education and outreach at The Thurber House, February 22, 2002.

Lentz, Ed. *As It Were: Stories of Old Columbus, vol. 2*. Red Mountain Press, 2001.

Thomas, Robert D., ed. *Columbus Unforgettables: A Collection of Columbus Yesterdays and Todays*. Robert D. Thomas, 1983.

The Thurber House Organ, Vol. 6 No. 2; Autumn 1988.

Woodyard, Chris. *Haunted Ohio: Ghostly Tales from the Buckeye State*. Kestrel Publications, Dayton, OH, 1991. Ninth printing, 2000.

The Man of Mystery

"Aged and eccentric recluse dies in his lonely 'castle,'" *The Columbus Citizen*. Tuesday, 12 May 1914, page 5.

Arter, Bill. *Columbus Vignettes, vol. 1*. Nida-Eckstein Printing, Inc., Columbus, OH, 1966.

Borne, Trish. "Supernatural sightings abound in The Villages," *Columbus This Week*, 29 October, 1990.

"Mayor to pick pallbearers for funeral of Dr. Schwartz," *The Columbus Citizen*. Wednesday, 13 May 1914, page 2.

Offense report OR49972E, Division of Police, Columbus, OH. December 2, 1956.

Offense report OR43139E, Division of Police, Columbus, OH. June 2, 1956.

Personal conversation with Chuck Bryan, January 15, 2002.

"Schwartz Castle Is Resold for $3755," *The Columbus Citizen*, August 7, 1915.

"Schwartz Castle Converted into Model Hospital," *The Columbus Sunday Dispatch*, November 4, 1917.

"Spooky Schwartz' Castle Holds Tales of 'Horror'," *Columbus Citizen-Journal*, November 23, 1967.

Switzer, John. "Spooky history surrounds old mansion," *The Columbus Dispatch*, Saturday, 22 May, 1993.

Thomas, Robert D., ed. *More Columbus Unforgettables: A Further Collection of Columbus Yesterdays and Todays*. Robert D. Thomas, 1986.

Woodyard, Chris. *Haunted Ohio III: Still More Ghostly Tales from the Buckeye State*. Kestrel Publications, Dayton, OH, 1994. Second printing, October 1995.

The Pink Lady

http://www.kappa.org/found.htm, March 27, 2002.

Arter, Bill. *Columbus Vignettes, vol. 1*. Nida-Eckstein Printing, Inc., Columbus, OH. 1966.

Interview with Kylie Towers, archivist/curator, Heritage Museum. April 4, 2002.

Samuelson, Robert E. et al. *Architecture: Columbus*. ©1976, The Foundation of The Columbus Chapter of the American Institute of Architects, Columbus, OH.

Thomas, Robert D., ed. *Columbus Unforgettables: A Collection of Columbus Yesterdays and Todays*. Robert D. Thomas, 1983.

The Grandpa Ghost

Story told by Beth Ervin in personal conversation, December 12, 2001.

The Restless Dead

Borne, Trish. "Supernatural sightings abound in The Villages," *The Villages ThisWeek*, October 29, 1990.

Lee, Alfred E., A.M. *History of the City of Columbus, Capital of Ohio, vol II*. Munsell & Co., New York and Chicago, 1892.

"Long after the sun goes down..." untitled article in *The Other Paper*, June 2, 1999.

Schlegel, Donald M. *The Columbus Catholic Cemetery: History and Records 1846–1874*. ©1983 by Donald M. Schlegel. Published by Columbus History Service, Columbus, OH, 1983.

Schlegel, Donald M. *The Columbus City Graveyards: Containing Histories of the Franklinton, North, East, South, and Colored Graveyards of Columbus, Ohio with a Consolidated List of all known Lot Owners, Burials, Inscriptions, and Removals*. Columbus History Service, Columbus, OH, 1985.

Studer, Jacob H. *Columbus, Ohio: Its History, Resources and Progress (Including Franklin County)*. 1873.

Williams, Brian. "Sewer work stops when workers find skeletal remains," *The Columbus Dispatch*, May 11, 2001.

Williams, Brian. "Sewer digging unearths more human skeletons," *The Columbus Dispatch*, May 16, 2001.

Williams, Brian. "Past comes to life as burial site is combed," *The Columbus Dispatch*, May 20, 2001.

The Return of Thurston

http://erh3.homestead.com/Magicians~ie4.html, May 7, 2002.

http://www.lookd.com/magic/emergence.html, May 7, 2002.

Foster, Dorothy Todd. "Test of Thurston's Pact at Crypt Fails," *Columbus Evening Dispatch*, April 13, 1937.

"He Tried...But Thurston's Spirit Didn't Hear," *The Columbus Citizen*, April 13, 1937.

Lentz, Ed. *As It Were: Stories of Old Columbus*, vol. 2. Red Mountain Press, 2001.

Stephens, Steve. "No good vibes from dead magician," *The Columbus Dispatch*, April 14, 1993.

"Thurston Rites Will Be Held Here Saturday," *Columbus Evening Dispatch*, April 14, 1936.

"Thurston Will Be Buried in Columbus, His Birthplace." *The Columbus Citizen*, April 14, 1936.

The Screams of the Dying

http://www.drc.state.oh.us/web/histop1/html, June 6, 2002. Reprint of "Inside the Pen," by David Lore, originally printed by *The Columbus Dispatch*, October 28, 1984.

http://www.ohiodeathrow.com, August 1, 2002. :The History of the Death Penalty."

"Chance photograph shows how rapidly pen fire spread..." *The Columbus Citizen*, April 25, 1930.

The Columbus Citizen (multiple stories), April 22, 1930.

Columbus Evening Dispatch (multiple stories), April 22, 1930.

Columbus Evening Dispatch (multiple stories), April 23, 1930.

Fogle, H.M. *The Palace of Death or The Ohio Penitentiary Annex*. Published by the author, Columbus, Ohio, 1908. Image clarified and copyrighted 1999 by Arthur W. McGraw.

Fornshell, Marvin E. *The Historical and Illustrated Ohio Penitentiary 1907–1908*. Image clarified and copyrighted 1997 by Arthur W. McGraw.

Lee, Alfred E., A.M. *History of the City of Columbus, Capital of Ohio, vol II*. Munsell & Co., New York and Chicago, 1892.

Lentz, Ed. *As It Were: Stories of Old Columbus*. Red Mountain Press, 1998.

Switzer, John. "Ghostly Tour Might Revive the Spirit of Halloween," *The Columbus Dispatch*, October 30, 1987.

Thomas, Robert D., ed. *Columbus Unforgettables: A Collection of Columbus Yesterdays and Todays*. Robert D. Thomas, 1983.

Thomas, Robert D., ed. *More Columbus Unforgettables: A Further Collection of Columbus Yesterdays and Todays*. Robert D. Thomas, 1986.

A Mansion Needs a Maid

Arter, Bill. *Columbus Vignettes, vol. 1*. Nida-Eckstein Printing, Inc., Columbus, OH. 1966.

"Beyond Incredible," *Ohio Magazine*, November 1980.

Borne, Trish. "Supernatural sightings abound in The Villages," *The Villages ThisWeek*, October 29, 1990.

Samuelson, Robert E. et al. *Architecture: Columbus*. ©1976, The Foundation of The Columbus Chapter of the American Institute of Architects, Columbus, OH.

Sterling, Lea Ann. *Historic Homes of Olde Towne, Columbus, Ohio*. Historic Homes of Olde Towne Coalition, 1999.

Woodyard, Chris. *Haunted Ohio II: More Ghostly Tales from the Buckeye State.* Kestrel Publications, Dayton, OH, 1992. Fourth printing, 1995.

Ghost Soldiers of Fort Hayes

Arter, Bill. *Columbus Vignettes, vol. 1.* Nida-Eckstein Printing, Inc., Columbus, OH. 1966.

Arter, Bill. *Columbus Vignettes, vol. 2.* Nida-Eckstein Printing, Inc., Columbus, OH. 1967.

Lentz, Ed. *As It Were: Stories of Old Columbus, vol. 2.* Red Mountain Press, 2001.

Switzer, John. "Fort Hayes ghosts await Halloween tours," *The Columbus Dispatch,* October 26, 1991.

Woodyard, Chris. *Haunted Ohio III: Still More Ghostly Tales from the Buckeye State.* Kestrel Publications, Dayton, OH, 1994. Second printing, October 1995.

The Castle Ghosts

Cole, Charles C. Jr. *A Fragile Capital: Identity and the Early Years of Columbus, Ohio.* Ohio State University Press, Columbus, Ohio, 2001.

"Esther's" story told during the Columbus Landmarks Ghost Tours, October 1996.

Personal story told by an instructor at the Cultural Arts Center, 1994.

Personal experience, 1994.

Phone statement from Jennifer Johnson, director of Cultural Arts Center, January 2002.

Lee, Alfred E., A.M. *History of the City of Columbus, Capital of Ohio, vol II.* Munsell & Co., New York and Chicago, 1892.

Lentz, Ed. *As It Were: Stories of Old Columbus.* Red Mountain Press, 1998.

Haunted Sites You Can Visit

Information was current at the time this book was published, but it is always a good idea to call ahead in case schedules have changed.

Camp Chase Confederate Cemetery

2900 Sullivant Avenue (just west of Hague Avenue)
Look for the stone wall topped with an iron rail. Park on a side street and walk a short distance, as there is no parking for the cemetery. Please remember that under Ohio law, cemeteries close at dusk.

Cultural Arts Center

139 West Main Street at Civic Center Drive
614-645-7047
There is metered parking across the street and on other nearby streets. Hours Mon.–Thurs. 8:30 a.m.–5 p.m., 7–10 p.m. for classes; Fri. 8:30 a.m.–5 p.m.; Sat.–Sun. 1–5 p.m.

The Elevator Brewery and Draught House

161 North High Street (between Long and Spring streets)
614-228-0500
There are metered parking spaces and parking garages nearby. Look for the distinctive curved stained glass facade. Hours: Mon.–Thurs. 11 a.m.–12 a.m., Fri. 11 a.m.–2 a.m., Sat. 5 p.m.–2 a.m. *www.elevatorbrewing.com*

Green Lawn Abbey

Greenlawn Avenue just west of Harmon Avenue
Although the mausoleum doors are generally kept locked, this is worth a look just from the outside. Continue west down Greenlawn Avenue to Green Lawn Cemetery, where many Columbus notables are buried, including the entire Kelton family, Frederick William Schwartz of Schwartz Castle, and James Thurber. Please respect Ohio law; cemeteries close at dusk.

Kappa Kappa Gamma Heritage Museum

530 E. Town Street
614-228-6515
Enter from the parking lot behind the house on Franklin Avenue. Open for tours Mon.–Fri., 10 a.m. –4 p.m. and on weekends by appointment.

Kelton House

586 E. Town Street
614-464-2022
Park on Town Street if you can find a space, or in the Junior League's lot behind the house off Franklin Avenue. Museum hours are Sundays from 1–4 p.m. Tours can be arranged at other times if scheduled in advance. $3 admission per adult; discounts for children and senior citizens.

The Ohio Penitentiary Site

Spring Street at Neil Avenue
The penitentiary was demolished in 1998 to clear the area for redevelopment, but most of the actual penitentiary site is still empty as this book is published. Contrary to rumors, Nationwide Arena does NOT sit atop the Old Pen; its footprint covered the parking area west of the CoreComm IceHaus, followed Neil Avenue to Spring Street, then west to the green space where the Union Depot arch stands today.

The Ohio Statehouse

Downtown between Broad, Third, State and High streets
614-728-2695, 1-888-OHIO-123
Pre-scheduled tours Mon.–Fri. 9:30 a.m.–3:15 p.m., beginning every 15 minutes. Walk-in tours begin at 10 a.m., 11:30 a.m., 2 p.m. and 3 p.m. weekdays. Weekend tours (both scheduled and walk-in) 11:15 a.m., 12:30 p.m., 2 p.m. and 3 p.m. Reservations are requested for groups of 10 or more. Please call to make your appointment; phone is answered from 8 a.m.–5 p.m.; voice mail is available at all other times.

Thurber House

77 Jefferson Avenue (between Broad and Long streets, west of I-71)
614-464-1032
Open to the public most afternoons, 12–4 p.m. Call for additional information.

More Ghosts and Columbus History

Want to find out more? Check these sources to start.

Ghost Books

● Chris Woodyard is the maven of Ohio ghost stories.

Woodyard, Chris. *The Ghost Hunter's Guide to Haunted Ohio.* Kestrel Publications, Dayton, OH, 2000.

Woodyard, Chris. *Haunted Ohio: Ghostly Tales from the Buckeye State.* Kestrel Publications, Dayton, OH, 1991.

Woodyard, Chris. *Haunted Ohio II: More Ghostly Tales from the Buckeye State.* Kestrel Publications, Dayton, OH, 1992.

Woodyard, Chris. *Haunted Ohio III: Still More Ghostly Tales from the Buckeye State.* Kestrel Publications, Dayton, OH, 1994.

Woodyard, Chris. *Haunted Ohio IV: Restless Spirits.* Kestrel Publications, Dayton, OH, 1997.

Woodyard, Chris. *Spooky Ohio: 13 Traditional Tales.* Kestrel Publications, Dayton, OH, 1995.

● Connie Cartmell weaves spooky tales from Marietta, the oldest permanent settlement in the old Northwest Territory.

Cartmell, Connie. *Ghosts of Marietta.* © 1996 by Connie Cartmell. Published by River Press and Connie Cartmell, 1996.

● Anne Oscard brings together female ghosts from the tri-state area.

Oscard, Anne. *Tristate Terrors.* ©1996 by Anne Oscard. Hermit Publications, Dayton, OH.

● Michael Norman and Beth Scott produced a number of good collections of ghost stories. This is their midwest collection.

Norman, Michael and Beth Scott. *Haunted Heartland.* Stanton & Lee, Madison, WI, © 1985.

Web Sites

● *Forgotten Ohio* • www.forgottenoh.com

This site has Ohio ghost stories as well as sections on Ohio cemeteries, abandoned buildings and structures, and ghost towns.*

● *The Ghosts of Ohio* • http://www.ghostsofohio.org/goo.htm

Lots of Ohio and nearby ghost stories. The Ghosts of Ohio is actually a not-for-profit group which was formed for the purpose of investigating ghosts scientifically. They are NOT "ghostbusters," but will investigate alleged hauntings.

● *Ghosts of the Prairie* • www.prairieghosts.com

The site of the American Ghost Society; ghost stories from all over, plus extensive information on ghost hunting. Also features an enormous catalog of ghost books from just about everywhere.

● *Invisible Ink: Books on Ghosts and Hauntings*™ • www.invink.com

Chris Woodyard's site features a large catalog of books as well as lots of general information about ghosts.

Please note that neither the author of Columbus Ghosts *nor Emuses Inc. encourages or condones illegal trespassing. However, this site is included for its truly fascinating content and historical information about several haunted sites.*

Columbus History Books

Arter, Bill. *Columbus Vignettes, vols. 1–6.* Nida-Eckstein Printing, Inc., Columbus, OH.

Clay, Paul, Patti Ongaro and Lois Neff, comp., *The Men and Women of Camp Chase.* The Hilltop Historical Society.

Cole, Charles C. Jr. *A Fragile Capital: Identity and the Early Years of Columbus, Ohio.* Ohio State University Press, Columbus, Ohio, 2001.

Henderson, Andrew. *Forgotten Columbus.* Copyright © 2002 by Andrew Henderson. Arcadia Press, an imprint of Tempus Publishing, Chicago, IL.

Lentz, Ed. *As It Were: Stories of Old Columbus.* Red Mountain Press 1998.

Lentz, Ed. *As It Were: Stories of Old Columbus, vol. 2.* Red Mountain Press, 2001.

Thomas, Robert D., ed. *Columbus Unforgettables: A Collection of Columbus Yesterdays and Todays.* Robert D. Thomas, 1983.

Thomas, Robert D., ed. *More Columbus Unforgettables: A Further Collection of Columbus Yesterdays and Todays.* Robert D. Thomas, 1986.

Libraries and Archives

The Columbus Metropolitan Library (Main Library)
> 96 South Grant Street • www.columbuslibrary.org
> 614-645-2275 (general) • 614-645-2710 (Biography, History & Travel)

The Ohio Historical Society Archives/Library
> I-71 and 17th Avenue (in the Ohio Historical Center)
> http://www.ohiohistory.org/resource/archlib/index.html
> 614-297-2510

The State Library of Ohio
> 274 East First Avenue • http://winslo.state.oh.us/
> 614-644-7061

Index

About the Author

Writer and designer Robin Smith has been collecting ghost stories since she was eleven years old. A lifelong resident of Ohio and a former *Ohio Magazine* staffer, she has collected a large number of stories and tons of Ohio trivia with which she torments her family and friends. She lives in the Columbus area with her husband Brian and daughter Jessica.

About the Publisher

Emuses Inc. was founded in December 2000 by writer and editor Jennifer E. Poleon and designers Kathy Murphy and Robin Smith. We specialize in publication design, including books, magazines and newsletters. Write us at

Emuses, Inc.
P.O. Box 1264
Worthington, OH 43085-1264

or e-mail us at

emuses@columbus.rr.com

Partial proceeds from this book will benefit The Columbus Landmarks Foundation.